WALKING THE GR5:
VOSGES
TO JURA

Titles in the Footpaths of Europe Series

Normandy and the Seine
Walking through Brittany
Walks in Provence
Coastal Walks: Normandy and Brittany
Walking the Pyrenees
Walks in the Auvergne
Walks in the Dordogne
Walks in the Loire Valley
Walking the GR5: Modane to Larche
Walking the GR5: Lake Geneva to Mont-Blanc
Paris to Boulogne
Walks in Corsica
Walking the GR5: Larche to Nice
Walking the GR5: Vosges to Jura
Walks in the Cévennes
Walks round Paris
Walking in France: The GR System

The publishers thank J. Cantaloube for permission to use his photographs in this book.

WALKING THE GR5: VOSGES TO JURA

Translated by Christine Wood
and Paul Becke

Robertson McCarta

The publishers thank the following people for their help with this book: Isabelle Daguin, Philippe Lambert, Serge Sineux.

First published in 1991 by

Robertson McCarta Limited
17-18 Angel Gate
City Road
London EC1V 2PT

in association with

Fédération Française de la Randonnée Pédestre
8 Avenue Marceau
75008 Paris

© Robertson McCarta Limited
© Fédération Française de Randonnée Pédestre
© Maps, Institut Geographique National (French Official Survey)
    and Robertson McCarta Limited.

Managing Editor Folly Marland
Series designed by Prue Bucknall
Production by Grahame Griffiths
Typeset by The Robertson Group, Llandudno
Origination by Toppan Limited
Planning Map by Rodney Paull

Printed in italy by Grafedit SpA, Bergamo.

British Library Cataloguing in Publication Data

Walking the GR5: Vosges to Jura. – (Footpaths of Europe).
    1. France. Alps – Visitors' guides
    I. Series
    914.48

    ISBN 1-85365-232-6

CONTENTS

The walks and maps

Walk 1   25

Walk 2   97

Walk 3 Tour du Pays de Montbéliard   .   144

Key to IGN Maps

Motorway, dual carriageway

Major road, four lanes or more

Main road, two-lane or three-lane, wide

Main road, two-lane, narrow

Narrow road, regularly surfaced

Other narrow road: regularly surfaced; irregularly surfaced

Field track, forest track, felling track, footpath

Track of disused road. Road under construction

Road through embankment, cutting. Tree-lined road or track

Bank. Hedge, line of trees

Railway: double track, single track. Electrified line. Station, waiting line. Halt, stop

Sidings or access lines. Narrow gauge line. Rack railway

Electricity transmission line. Cable railway. Ski lift

National boundary with markers

Boundary and administrative centre of department, district

Boundary and administrative centre of canton, commune

Boundary of military camp, firing range

Boundary of State forest, National Park, outer zone of National Park

Triangulation points

Church, chapel, shrine. Cross, tomb, religious statue. Cemetery

Watch tower, fortress. Windmill, wind-pump. Chimney

Storage tank: oil, gas. Blast furnace. Pylon. Quarry

Cave. Monument, pillar. Castle. Ruins

Megalithic monument: dolmen, menhir. Viewpoint. Campsite

Market-hall, shed, glasshouse, casemate

Access to underground workings. Refuge. Ski-jump

Population/thousands

Bridge. Footbridge. Ford. Ferry

Lake, pool. Area liable to flooding. Marsh

Source, spring. Well, water-tank. Water-tower, reservoir

Watercourse lined with trees. Waterfall. Dam. Dyke

Navigable canal, feeder or irrigator. Lock, machine-operated. Underground channel

Contour lines. 10 m. interval. Hollow. Small basin. Scree

Principal — Secondary

Possibly private or controlled access

For shooting times, go to town hall or gendarmerie

PF   SP

CT   C

183,2   0,4   0,15   0,06

Ch.ᵃᵘ d'Eau

Woodland   Scrub   Orchard, plantation   Vines   Ricefield

All maps are IGN Orange series. 1:50 000

© I.G.N. – Paris

6

A note from the publisher

The books in this French Walking Guide series are produced in association and with the help of the Fédération Française de la Randonnée Pédestre (French ramblers' association) — generally known as the FFRP.

The FFRP is a federal organisation and is made up of regional, local and many other associations and bodies that form its constituent parts. Individual membership is through these various local organisations. The FFRP therefore acts as an umbrella organisation overseeing the waymarking of footpaths, training and the publishing of the Topoguides, detailed guides to the Grande Randonnée footpaths.

There are at present about 170 Topoguides in print, compiled and written by local members of the FFRP, who are responsible for waymarking the walks — so they are well researched and accurate.

We have translated the main itinerary descriptions, amalgamating and adapting several Topoguides to create new regional guides. We have retained the basic Topoguide structure, indicating length and times of walks, and the Institut Géographique National (official French survey) maps overlaid with the routes.

The information contained in this guide is the latest available at the time of going to print. However, as publishers we are aware that this kind of information is continually changing and we are anxious to enhance and improve the guides as much as possible. We encourage you to send us suggestions, criticisms and those little bits of information you may wish to share with your fellow walkers. Our address is: Robertson McCarta, 17-18 Angel Gate, City Road, London EC1V 2PT.

We shall be happy to offer a free copy of any one of these books to any reader whose suggestions are subsequently incorporated into a new edition.

It is possible to create a variety of routes by referring to the walks in the contents page and to the planning map (inside the front cover). Transport is listed in the alphabetical index in the back of the book and there is an accommodation guide.

The full range of IGN (French OS) maps is available from The Map and Guide Shop, who operate a mail order service, 17-18 Angel Gate, City Road, London EC1V 2PT, Tel: 071 278 8276

KEY

Gournay

This example shows that you can expect the walk from Gournay to Arbois to take 2 hours, 10 minutes.

2:10

ARBOIS
⌂ ⌂ ✕ ⚎ ▭
14th century church

Arbois has a variety of facilities, including hotels and buses. Hotel addresses and bus/train connections may be listed in the index at the back of the book.

A grey arrow indicates an alternative route that leaves and returns to the main route.

Detour

indicates a short detour off the route to a town with facilities or to an interesting sight.

Symbols:

⌂ hotel
⌂ youth hostel, hut or refuge
⚑ camping
✕ restaurant
♇ cafe

⚎ shops
▬ railway station
▭ buses
⛴ ferry
ℤ tourist information

8

THE FOOTPATHS OF FRANCE

by Robin Neillands

Why should you go walking in France? Well, walking is fun and as for France, Danton summed up the attractions of that country with one telling phrase: 'Every man has two countries,' he said, 'his own . . . and France.' That is certainly true in my case and I therefore consider it both a pleasure and an honour to write this general introduction to these footpath guides to France. A pleasure because walking in or through France is my favourite pastime, an honour because these excellent English language guides follow in the course set by those Topoguides published in French by the Fédération Française pour la Randonnée Pédestre, which set a benchmark for quality that all footpath guides might follow. Besides, I believe that good things should be shared and walking in France is one of the most pleasant activities I know.

I have been walking in France for over thirty years. I began by rambling — or rather ambling — through the foothills of the Pyrenees, crossing over into Spain past the old Hospice de France, coming back over the Somport Pass in a howling blizzard, which may account for the fact that I totally missed two sets of frontier guards on both occasions. Since then I have walked in many parts of France and even from one end of it to the other, from the Channel to the Camargue, and I hope to go on walking there for many years to come.

The attractions of France are legion, but there is no finer way to see and enjoy them than on foot. France has two coasts, at least three mountain ranges — the Alps, Pyrenees and the Massif Central — an agreeable climate, a great sense of space, good food, fine wines and, believe it or not, a friendly and hospitable people. If you don't believe me, go there on foot and see for yourself. Walking in France will appeal to every kind of walker, from the day rambler to the backpacker, because above all, and in the nicest possible way, the walking in France is well organised, but those Francophiles who already know France well will find it even more pleasurable if they explore their favourite country on foot.

The GR system

The Grande Randonnée (GR) footpath network now consists of more than 40,000 kilometres (25,000 miles) of long-distance footpath, stretching into every part of France, forming a great central sweep around Paris, probing deeply into the Alps, the Pyrenees, and the volcanic cones of the Massif Central. This network, the finest system of footpaths in Europe, is the creation of that marvellously named organisation, *la Fédération Française de Randonnée Pédestre, Comité National des Sentiers de Grande Randonnée,* which I shall abbreviate to FFRP-CNSGR. Founded in 1948, and declaring that, *'un jour de marche, huit jours de santé* the FFRP-CNSGR has flourished for four decades and put up the now familiar red-and-white waymarks in every corner of the country. Some of these footpaths are classic walks, like the famous GR65, *Le Chemin de St. Jacques,* the ancient Pilgrim Road to Compostela, the TMB, the *Tour du Mont Blanc,* which circles the mountain through France, Switzerland and Italy, or the 600-mile long GR3, the *Sentier de la Loire,* which runs from the Ardèche to the Atlantic, to give three examples from the hundred or so GR trails available. In addition there is an abundance of GR du Pays or regional footpaths, like the *Sentier de la Haute Auvergne,* and the *Sentier Tour des Monts d'Aubrac.* A 'Tour' incidentally, is usually a circular walk.

Many of these regional or provincial GR trails are charted and waymarked in red-and-yellow by local outdoor organisations such as ABRI (Association Bretonne des Relais et Itineraires) for Brittany, or CHAMINA for the Massif Central. The walker in France will soon become familiar with all these footpath networks, national, regional or local, and find them the perfect way into the heart and heartland of France. As a little bonus, the GR networks are expanding all the time, with the detours — or *varientes* — off the main route eventually linking with other GR paths or *varientes* and becoming GR trails in their own right.

Walkers will find the GR trails generally well marked and easy to follow, and they have two advantages over the footpaths commonly encountered in the UK. First, since they are laid out by local people, they are based on intricate local knowledge of the local sights. If there is a fine view, a mighty castle or a pretty village on your footpath route, your footpath through France will surely lead you to it. Secondly, all French footpaths are usually well provided with a wide range of comfortable country accommodation, and you will discover that the local people, even the farmers, are well used to walkers and greet them with a smile, a *'Bonjour'* and a *'bonne route'.*

Terrain and Climate

As a glance at these guides or any Topoguide will indicate, France has a great variety of terrain. France is twice the size of the UK and many natural features are also on a larger scale. There are three main ranges of mountains, the Alps contain the highest mountain in Europe, the Pyrenees go up to 10,000 ft, the Massif Central peaks to over 6000 ft, and there are many similar ranges with hills which overtop our highest British peak, Ben Nevis. On the other hand, the Auvergne and the Jura have marvellous open ridge walking, the Cévennes are steep and rugged, the Ardèche and parts of Provence are hot and wild, the Île de France, Normandy, Brittany and much of western France is green and pleasant, not given to extremes. There is walking in France for every kind of walker, but given such a choice the wise walker will consider the complications of terrain and weather before setting out, and go suitably equipped.

France enjoys three types of climate: continental, oceanic, and Mediterranean. South of the Loire it will certainly be hot to very hot from mid-April to late September. Snow can fall on the mountains above 4000 ft from mid-October and last until May, or even lie year-round on the tops and in couloirs; in the high hills an ice-axe is never a frill. I have used one by the Brèche de Roland in the Pyrenees in mid-June.

Wise walkers should study weather maps and forecasts carefully in the week before they leave for France, but can generally expect good weather from May to October, and a wide variety of weather — the severity depending on the terrain — from mid-October to late Spring.

Accommodation

The walker in France can choose from a wide variety of accommodation with the assurance that the walker will always be welcome. This can range from country hotels to wild mountain pitches, but to stay in comfort, many walkers will travel light and overnight in the comfortable hotels of the *Logis de France* network.

Logis de France: The *Logis de France* is a nationwide network of small, family-run country hotels, offering comfortable accommodation and excellent food. *Logis* hotels are graded and can vary from a simple, one-star establishment, with showers and linoleum, to a four- or five-star *logis* with gastronomic menus and deep-pile carpets. All offer excellent value for money, and since there are over 5,000 scattered across the French countryside, they provide a good focus for a walking day. An annual guide to the *Logis* is available from the French Government Tourist Office, 178 Piccadilly, London W1V 0AL, Tel (071) 491 7622.

Gîtes d'étape: A *gîte d'étape* is best imagined as an unmanned youth hostel for outdoor folk of all ages. They lie along the footpath networks and are usually signposted or listed in the guides. They can be very comfortable, with bunk beds, showers, a well equipped kitchen, and in some cases they have a warden, a *gardien,* who may offer meals. *Gîtes d'étape* are designed exclusively for walkers, climbers, cyclists, cross country skiers or horse-riders. A typical price (1990) would be Fr.25 for one night. *Gîtes d'étape* should not be confused with a *Gîte de France.* A *gîte* — usually signposted as 'Gîte de France' — is a country cottage available for a holiday let, though here too, the owner may be more than willing to rent it out as overnight accommodation.

Youth hostels: Curiously enough, there are very few Youth Hostels in France outside the main towns. A full list of the 200 or so available can be obtained from the Youth Hostel Association (YHA), Trevelyan House, St. Albans, Herts AL1 2DY.

Pensions or cafes: In the absence of an hotel, a *gîte d'étape* or a youth hostel, all is not lost. France has plenty of accommodation and an enquiry at the village cafe or bar will usually produce a room. The cafe/hotel may have rooms or suggest a nearby pension or a *chambre d'hôte.* Prices start at around Fr.50 for a room, rising to say, Fr.120. (1990 estimate).

Chambres d'hôte: A *chambre d'hôte* is a guest room, or, in English terms, a bed-and-breakfast, usually in a private house. Prices range from about Fr.90 a night. *Chambres d'hôte* signs are now proliferating in the small villages of France and especially if you can speak a little French are an excellent way to meet the local people. Prices (1990) are from, say, Fr.70 for a room, not per person.

Abris: Abris, shelters or mountain huts can be found in the mountain regions, where they are often run by the Club Alpin Français, an association for climbers. They range from the comfortable to the primitive, are often crowded and are sometimes reserved for members. Details from the Club Alpin Français, 7 Rue la Boétie, Paris 75008, France.

Camping: French camp sites are graded from one to five star, but are generally very good at every level, although the facilities naturally vary from one cold tap to shops, bars and heated pools. Walkers should not be deterred by the *'Complet'* (Full) sign on the gate or office window: a walker's small tent will usually fit in somewhere. *Camping à la ferme,* or farm camping, is increasingly popular, more primitive — or less regimented — than the official sites, but widely available and perfectly adequate. Wild camping is officially not permitted in National Parks, but unofficially if you are over 1,500m away from a road, one hour's walk from a *gîte* or camp site, and where possible ask permission, you should have no trouble. French country people will always assist the walker to find a pitch.

The law for walkers
The country people of France seem a good deal less concerned about their 'rights' than the average English farmer or landowner. I have never been ordered off land in France or greeted with anything other than friendliness . . . maybe I've been lucky. As

a rule, walkers in France are free to roam over all open paths and tracks. No decent walker will leave gates open, trample crops or break down walls, and taking fruit from gardens or orchards is simply stealing. In some parts of France there are local laws about taking chestnuts, mushrooms (and snails), because these are cash crops. Signs like *Réserve de Chasse,* or *Chasse Privée* indicate that the shooting is reserved for the landowner. As a general rule, behave sensibly and you will be tolerated everywhere, even on private land.

The country code
Walkers in France should obey the Code du Randonneur.

- Love and respect nature.
- Avoid unnecessary noise.
- Destroy nothing.
- Do not leave litter.
- Do not pick flowers or plants.
- Do not disturb wildlife.
- Re-close all gates.
- Protect and preserve the habitat.
- No smoking or fires in the forests. (This rule is essential and is actively enforced by foresters and police.)
- Respect and understand the country way of life and the country people.
- Think of others as you think of yourself.

Transport
Transportation to and within France is generally excellent. There are no less than nine Channel ports: Dunkirk, Calais, Boulogne, Dieppe, Le Havre, Caen/Ouistreham, Cherbourg, Saint-Malo and Roscoff, and a surprising number of airports served by direct flights from the UK. Although some of the services are seasonal, it is often possible to fly direct to Toulouse, Poitiers, Nantes, Perpignan, Montpellier, indeed to many provincial cities, as well as Paris and such obvious destinations as Lyon and Nice. Within France the national railway, the SNCF, still retains a nationwide network. Information, tickets and a map can be obtained from the SNCF. France also has a good country bus service and the *gare routière* is often placed just beside the railway station. Be aware though, that many French bus services only operate within the *département*, and they do not generally operate from one provincial city to the next. I cannot encourage people to hitch-hike, which is both illegal and risky, but walkers might consider a taxi for their luggage. Almost every French village has a taxi driver who will happily transport your rucksacks to the next night-stop, fifteen to twenty miles away, for Fr.50 a head or even less.

Money
Walking in France is cheap, but banks are not common in the smaller villages, so carry a certain amount of French money and the rest in traveller's cheques or Eurocheques, which are accepted everywhere.

Clothing and equipment
The amount of clothing and equipment you will need depends on the terrain, the length of the walk, the time of your visit, the accommodation used. Outside the mountain areas it is not necessary to take the full range of camping or backpacking gear. I once

walked across France from the Channel to the Camargue along the Grande Randonneé footpaths in March, April and early May and never needed to use any of the camping gear I carried in my rucksack because I found hotels everywhere, even in quite small villages.

Essential items are:
In summer: light boots, a hat, shorts, suncream, lip salve, mosquito repellent, sunglasses, a sweater, a windproof cagoule, a small first-aid kit, a walking stick.
In winter: a change of clothing, stormproof outer garments, gaiters, hat, lip salve, a companion.
In the mountains at any time: large-scale maps (1:25,000), a compass, an ice-axe. In winter, add a companion and ten-point crampons.
At any time: a phrase book, suitable maps, a dictionary, a sense of humour.

The best guide to what to take lies in the likely weather and the terrain. France tends to be informal, so there is no need to carry a jacket or something smart for the evenings. I swear by Rohan clothing, which is light, smart and functional. The three things I would never go without are light, well-broken-in boots and several pairs of loop-stitched socks, and my walking stick.

Health hazards:
Health hazards are few. France can be hot in summer, so take a full water-bottle and refill at every opportunity. A small first-aid kit is sensible, with plasters and 'mole-skin' for blisters, but since prevention is better than the cure, loop-stitched socks and flexible boots are better. Any French chemist — *a pharmacie* — is obliged to render first-aid treatment for a small fee. These pharmacies can be found in most villages and large towns and are marked by a green cross.

Dogs are both a nuisance and a hazard. All walkers in France should carry a walking stick to fend off aggressive curs. Rabies — *la rage* — is endemic and anyone bitten must seek immediate medical advice. France also possesses two types of viper, which are common in the hill areas of the south. In fairness, although I found my walking stick indispensable, I must add that in thirty years I have never even seen a snake or a rabid dog. In case of real difficulty, dial 17 for the police and the ambulance.

Food and wine
One of the great advantages with walking in France is that you can end the day with a good meal and not gain an ounce. French country cooking is generally excellent and good value for money, with the price of a four-course menu starting at about Fr.45. The ingredients for the mid-day picnic can be purchased from the village shops and these also sell wine. Camping-Gaz cylinders and cartridges are widely available, as is 2-star petrol for stoves. Avoid naked fires.

Preparation
The secret of a good walk lies in making adequate preparations before you set out. It pays to be fit enough to do the daily distance at the start. Much of the necessary information is contained in this guide, but if you need more, look in guidebooks or outdoor magazines, or ask friends.

The French

I cannot close this introduction without saying a few words about the French, not least because the walker in France is going to meet rather more French people than, say, a motorist will, and may even meet French people who have never met a foreigner before. It does help if the visitor speaks a little French, even if only to say *'bonjour'* and *'Merci'* and *'S'il vous plait'*. The French tend to be formal so it pays to be polite, to say 'hello', to shake hands. I am well aware that relations between France and England have not always been cordial over the last six hundred years or so, but I have never met with hostility of any kind in thirty years of walking through France. Indeed, I have always found that if the visitor is prepared to meet the French halfway, they will come more than halfway to greet him or her in return, and are both friendly and hospitable to the passing stranger.

As a final tip, try smiling. Even in France, or especially in France, a smile and a *'pouvez-vous m'aider?'* (Can you help me?) will work wonders. That's my last bit of advice, and all I need do now is wish you *'Bonne Route'* and good walking in France.

THE GR5

by Henri Viaux

President of the French Ramblers Association,1977-1989

The systematic development of long-distance walking in France dates from the immediate post-war period, when two important societies - the Touring Club de France and the Club Alpin Français - began using substantial numbers of volunteers to establish a network of footpaths covering the whole country. These routes became known as 'Sentiers de Grande Randonnée' - 'long-distance footpaths' - soon abbreviated to the simple title of 'GR', each linear or circular route having its own identifying number. The principal aim of the GR paths was to make the best possible use of paths and tracks barred to motorised vehicles, and to reveal rural France in all its richness and variety - the natural wealth of upland and lowland landscapes, the human interest of traditional rural life, and the inherited magnificence of buildings and monuments - combined with enjoyable physical activity. France's mountains have naturally provided an important element of the network. Standardised waymarking was designed to encourage familiarity and confidence in walking: the markings consist of two bars, one red and one white, painted on to any permanent feature along the route.

One of the first footpaths to be planned and established was the GR5, crossing the whole of eastern France from the Luxembourg frontier to the Mediterranean coast on the Côte d'Azur, via the principal mountain massifs - the Vosges, Jura, and the Alps. The route was later extended through Belgium to Ostend.

Completion of the route took a long time, but the most important section, across the Alps - already well-known to climbers, and using traditional tracks familiar to shepherds, itinerant traders, and armies on the march - was soon mapped out and established. The Savoy section of the GR5 was opened to walkers in 1955, extending in due course to Nice and Menton on the Côte d'Azur.

Complementary circular routes were established at the same time in the main mountain massifs, enabling walkers to explore the remote inner mountain areas in greater detail. These too are important GR routes; from north to south, they are: the Tour du Mont-Blanc, across the Vanoise (GR55), the Ecrins - Oisans massif (GR54), the Queyras massif (GR58), the Ubaye massif (GR56), and the Mercantour (GR52).

All these GR routes follow moderate mountain altitudes, between approximately 1,000 and 1,500 metres; any reasonably fit walker can thus explore these great mountain areas without the need for specialised mountaineer equipment. The footpaths lead from col to col and valley to valley, through villages and hamlets where the traditional rural pattern of mountain life still persists almost unchanged: in the mountains it is nature - topography and climate - which commands, and mankind who obeys. Conditions are hard at these high altitudes, demanding endurance and experience and not suited to everyone in primitive huts alongside the flocks in their alpine pastures. For the urban holiday-maker who walks these paths, the encounter with such a way of life can be enlightening and thought-provoking. Nature too has much to reveal to the visitor; summer months bring the delights of flowering alpine meadows, inspiration of the 'mille-fleurs' tapestries. Animal and bird life in the mountains is no less fascinating, for those who are prepared to get up early and go equipped with a good pair of binoculars and plenty of patience: marmots, chamois and ibex can all be seen at various stages along the route, there may be rare birds such as eagles and grouse, the choughs, finches, and many forms of passerines are commonplace. In autumn walkers can enjoy wild raspberries, bilberries, and mushrooms.

Walking the GR5 and its branches demands a sound pair of lungs and good leg muscles; and will specially interest those with a lively curiosity concerning all aspects of nature - though few could walk such a route without being fascinated by its flora and geological structure, and its resident animal life.

Romantic writers of the mid-nineteenth century who discovered the Chamonix Valley, the gateway to the upper Alps, spoke of 'these sublime and terrible mountains'. Human attitudes to the mountains have changed since then, and no-one now would dare to call them terrible; but for the walker who follows the GR5 on a fine summer's day, past majestic rock faces, snow-fields and towering glaciers, the mountains remain truly sublime.

The Alpine GR5, North

The northern Alpine section of the GR5 goes through the départements of Haute-Savoie and Savoie, making up the historic province of Savoy which in 1860 voted to become part of France. This is the region of the true Alps, with Mont Blanc their highest peak. The GR5 crosses the area at a relatively modest altitude; starting from Lake Geneva (Lac Léman), the path climbs gently up through the Chablais meadows to the Col d'Anterne, its first high pass. The descent through the Chamonix valley reveals the magnificent ensemble of the Mont Blanc massif; the path curves round to the west of Mont Blanc, southwards to the Vanoise massif and its National Park. Along the way two mountains - from the Tarentaise valley to the Maurienne valley. From the latter the path climbs up to the Vallée Etroite which marks the climatic frontier of the southern Alps.

On its way the GR5 shares its route for some way with the internationally famous Tour du Mont-Blanc GR, which crosses various cols at or above an altitude of 2,500 metres and runs into Italy and Switzerland, with extraordinary views of the great faces and glaciers of the roof of Europe. The route through the Col de Balme to Brévent via the Balcon de la Flégère is one of the most impressive in the whole Alpine massif.

The Alpine GR5, South

On leaving Savoy the GR5 goes over the Col de la Vallée Etroite, the climatic threshold of the southern Alps. Here it embarks on a series of mountainous massifs slightly lower than the northern Alps and offering less austere landscapes with the welcoming Névache valley as a typical introductory example. Next the route crosses the Regional Nature Park of the Queyras massif; it is rewarding to turn off at Saint-Véran or Ceillac to walk the GR58 which explores all areas of the National Park.

After crossing the Ubaye massif and the Haute-Tinée, the GR5 enters the National Park of the Mercantour massif in Haute Provence; here it divides in two, one branch leading to Nice and the other to Menton with distant views over the Mediterranean. Here too there is good reason to make a detour, to enjoy the newly established GR of the Mercantour Panorama.

First, however, the GR5 passes the Ecrins National Park, to the left and on a level with Briançon. The Ecrins Park has two important, circular GR routes: the high mountain GR54 path, demanding and occasionally bleak, dominated by impressive rock faces including La Meije; and the GR50, the Tour du Haut-Dauphiné, less strenuous, but offering magnificent glimpses of the high Ecrins peaks.

Regional Nature Park of the Ballons des Vosges.

The 25th French Park, created on June 4th 1989, is crossed by the GR5 from north to south. It covers an area of 3,000km^2, and comprises the whole of the upper Rhine valleys from Saint-Marie-aux-Mines to Masevaux, the Franche-Comté Vosges including the Mille-Étangs, the piedmonts of the Ballon d'Alsace and the High Valleys of the Vosges département. The purpose of the Ballons des Vosges Regional Nature Park, is to maintain a fair balance between the preservation of natural and cultural resources and local economic development.

Exploring the Ballons des Vosges Regional Nature Park by the GR5 offers a wide variety of landscape, natural environment and human habitation along the 150km from Thannenkirch to Giromagny.

The keen observer along this route may appreciate two attributes which in part contributed to the creation of the Regional Nature Park: the diversity of plantlife; and the richness of its wildlife.

Vegetation

Within the area of the park, there are exceptionally varied forested and open areas. The GR5 route passes through four types of forest vegetation, characteristic of the Vosges Mountains.

- The hill type, from 500m-700m, in the wine growing and agricultural area, where oaks predominate.
- The mountain type, from 700m-1100m, where resinous pine trees mingle with beeches.
- The subalpine type, from 1,100m-1,200m, with no pine trees, features beech groves, among other broadleaf trees such as maple and mountain ash.
- Above 1,200m, the natural tree line, is the subalpine grassland, the high haulms, where you find many alpine or subarctic plants, such as mat-grass, the alpine anemone, the Vosges pansy, the heathers, bilberry, crowberry, red bilberry, and the megaphorbeae, aconites and alpine mulgedea.

Due to the prevailing winds, on the west slope of the high Vosges, there are peat bogs, damp places resulting from the slow accumulation of peat which have to this day preserved traces of flora from colder periods, droseras, linaigrettes, marsh bilberry.

Wildlife

In the Regional Nature Park, the wildlife still lives in a varied, rich natural habitat. The Vosges forests doubtless constitute the most varied areas and provide favourable habitats for many species: red and roe deer, boar, chamois which sometimes feed on saplings and young trees.

Small carnivores such as wild cats, martens, badgers, and foxes live there, but they are rarely seen. Since 1983, the lynx which was exterminated two centuries ago, has come back to complete the range of wildlife.

There are also many birds and they illustrate the highland or northern character of the Vosges forests. The woodpecker, goshawk, hazel hen, nut cracker, crossbill, and ring ouzel frequent the mixed forest. Among the most notable species are the capercaillie, symbol of the Vosges forests, and without doubt one of the most demanding birds. The causes of its rarity are directly linked to changes in its habitat, affecting its tranquillity, composition and appearance.

At the summit of the Vosges, on the heathland or the peat, one can observe a whole series of the most common birds, the lark, the yellow-hammer, and more rarely the alpine pipit, the raven, the snowfinch, the Teng-malm owl. Mammals are equally well

represented by the marten, the ermine and the hare. Since it was introduced in 1956, the chamois has perhaps become the most characteristic species of the great Vosges Ridge.

The Regions Covered

The Vosges
The GR53 and GR5 paths leaving Wissembourg, cross the Northern, Middle and Southern Vosges, to reach Fesches-le-Châtel, beyond the Porte de Bourgogne (or Trouée de Belfort), at the foot of the Jura. They go through a variety of areas which need introduction.

Geology
The Northern Vosges stretch from Wissembourg to the Col de Saverne. Of moderate altitude, their highest point is the Grand-Wintersberg at 581m. They were mildly uplifted following the alpine folding and are composed of layers of sandstone cut into deep valleys, where erosion has sculpted heights in tabular or rounded form covered with forests. Erosion has left outstanding the most resistant parts of the sandstone rocks, giving these steep slopes with their many fortresses, a ruined, romantic aspect.

They are not very wide at the Wissembourg height and the mountain narrows at the Col de Saverne where it is only 4 kilometres wide, and 410 metres high.

We pass on to the Middle Vosges, whose base formed of gneiss and granite, disappears under the sandstone of the secondary period, forming summits which are not very high initially and gain in height to about 1,009m at Donon, and 1,100m at the granite outcrop of the Champ du Feu, before sloping down to Val-de-Villé.

Beyond Haut-Koenigsbourg, we get into the Hautes-Vosges, or crystalline Vosges, where the rocks, gneiss and granite among others, date from the primary period. Strongly uplifted in the tertiary period by the alpine folding, these landscapes were carved out by erosion from the meltwaters of glaciers in the quaternary period, with their alpine forms, like the deeply cut rocks, the steep sloped or even U-shaped valleys, the cirque lakes and moraines. Heights climb to the order of 1,200 to 1,300m: it is in this part of the Vosges that we find the highest point, the Grand Ballon, at 1,424m. Finally, after descending from the Ballon d'Alsace in the Belfort region, you cross a landscape with valleys cut into it, the Porte de Bourgogne, the transition between the basins of the Rhône and the Rhine, between the Vosges and the Jura.

The Alsace slope of the Vosges is steep; it corresponds to the fault line marking the collapse of the Rhine Fault. Hills covered with loess and marl run from north to south and form the transition to the Plain of Alsace. The rivers flow to the east, towards the Rhine. The most important of them are the Sauer, the Zinsel du Nord, the Zorn, the Mossig, the Bruche, the Giessen, the Fecht, the Lauch, the Thur and the Doller.

The Fortresses
The ancient Hohenbourg fortress was built towards the end of the 12th century by the Puller family. They were citizens of Strasbourg who later took the name of Puller de Hohenbourg. The Puller family died out in 1482 and the château passed to Schweighard de Sickingen, husband of Marguerite de Hohenboug and father of the

famous François de Sickingen. In the second half of the 16th century the château was restored in the renaissance style. It was destroyed by Montclar in 1689, during the wars of Louis XIV.

The Château of Fleckenstein was once one of the greatest, strongest and most magnificent fortresses of the Vosges, with staircases, wells, stables and halls hewn out of the rock. The château is built on a huge sandstone rock 40m high, 50m long but only 6 to 8m wide. It was first occupied by Godfried de Fleckenstein in 1129.

From the end of the 13th century, the Fleckensteins were part of the aristocracy and owned vast lands which stretched as far as the Rhine. There were three branches of this family whose members often occupied important posts. Some were Haguenau imperial bailiffs, others were in the Church. In the 15th century one was Bishop of Worms, another Bishop of Basle. The family died out in 1720. The château was destroyed by Montclar about 1680.

The Château of Froensbourg was built about the middle of the 13th century by the Lords of Froensbourg, relatives of the Fleckensteins. It was destroyed in 1369 by the Bishop of Strasbourg's troops because the lords were brigands. Later the Barons of Fleckenstein acquired and restored it. Like all the châteaux of the region it was destroyed by Montclar's troops about 1680.

The Château of Wasigenstein was founded in 788 with the name Wassenstein. You can see two châteaux built on rocks and separated by a deep moat. They date from the beginning of the 13th century.

The Château of Vieux-Windstein is thought to be a Celtic or Roman fortification. Two huge monoliths rise from the rock, with halls, dungeons, wells and passages hewn out of the rock. The château was built at the beginning of the 13th century by Pierre, Abbot of Neubourg. It belonged to the Windstein family from 1216 and was destroyed in 1332 because the lords were brigands. It then passed to the Durkheim family. It was partially destroyed in the Peasants War in 1525 and played only a small part beside Nouveau Windstein until its destruction by Montclar in 1680.

The ancient fortress of Nouveau Windstein was built in 1340 by Guillaume de Windstein. At the end of the 14th century and beginning of the 15th, the château belonged jointly to the Windstein, Lichtenberg, Linange and Durkheim families. In 1471 the Durkheim family became the sole owner. During the Thirty Years War the château stood firm against Maréchal Vaubrun's attacks but fell when bombarded by Montclar's artillery in 1680. The château is famous for its knights' hall and a fine ogive window with niches and benches. It has a huge cellar hewn out of the rock.

The Château of Wasenbourg was first mentioned in 751. It was built on the site of an ancient Roman fort in 1273 by Conrad de Lichtenberg, Bishop of Strasbourg. You can see the signs of the masons and sculptors of Strasbourg Cathedral on the stones. There are some remains of fine architecture. A bay with eight small columns in pure gothic style divides the opening into nine narrow ogive windows decorated with seven rose windows all with delicate tracery. To the right lie the ruins of Wachtfelsen, a Roman look-out post. There are remnants of a temple dedicated to Mercury.

The Château of Grand Arnsbourg was built in the 12th century by the Landgraves of Alsace. It was partially destroyed in 1525 during the Peasants War and completely destroyed in 1680 by Montclar's troops. It is accessible only by ladder. There is a fine view over the valley of the North Zinsel and the Château of Lichtenberg.

The Château of la Petite-Pierre, was called Castrum Lutzelenstein from 1223. It was a stronghold of the Bishop of Strasbourg and changed hands several times. The present château dates from 1566. The little walled town grew up around it. The church of 1417 is in late gothic style. The nave and the tower were renovated in 1884-85.

There are some interesting tombstones.

Jura

In contrast to the countless hils and valleys of the Vosges to the north, and to the peerless grandeur of the Alps to the south, the Jura is characterised by high plateaux and deep gorges. Only recently has this section of the GR5 been adequately waymarked.

Several distinct areas of this isolated region can be identified. The north's low plateaux of the Montbéliard hinterland with its imposing oak and beech forests are followed, between Charmauvillers and Villers-le-Lac, by the Doubs Gorfes. The final part of the walk leads to the magnificent panorama from Mont d'Or at 1,463 metres and the long descent towards Mouthe, through the forests and pastures of Le Risoux.

In winter, the Haut-Jura is traditionally the land of cold and snow. From St-Claude to Maiche, from Delemont to Saint-Cergue, the 'montagnons' are only happy when winter really means winter.

The walker will find the Comtois farms, located at the edge of the forests, to be solidly built to withstand the rigours of winter. And it was in these farms that Jura clockmaking, which is now the prime activity of most villages, was first perfected. Another symbol of the harmonious relationship between man and nature in the Jura is the village creamery, where Comté gruyère is produced.

The Jura House and its 'Tué'

In the Jura mountains, the winters are harsh: the snow and the cold are realities which have to be taken seriously. The whole organization of the rural house is affected by it: the dwelling, cowshed, barn and sheds are contained within a square under one roof.

Its architectural design meets specific requirements to be resistant to low temperatures and damp. The thickness of the walls and smallness of the openings are a solution to this problem. Only the entrance door to the cowshed really gives an indication of the front of the house. The walls, made from large limestone blocks and lined with rough-cast, are protected by the roof overhang, sending the rain and snow further away. Entry to the barn is usually through the rear, an earth bank enabling hay-carts to be brought right up to the door step. The great stock of forage needed for the cattle during the winter gives the building insulation against the cold.

In the past, the *couvert,* an immense roof covering the building, used to be made of wooden planks, or *esols.* Of spruce or fir and cut with the grain of the wood, they overlapped each other, and were completely watertight. Today, the roofs are mostly of tiles or steel plates. Though not obvious from the outside of the house, the *tué* chimney is a key feature of house construction in this region. More than a chimney, it is really a partitioned room, the *tcha*, the kitchen occupying the centre of the dwelling and communicating with the bedrooms, cowshed and barn. The fireplace, situated in the middle of the room, distributes the heat to the whole of the house, and the smoke escapes through a monumental chimney-top.

It was in this *tué* that, in former times, the quarters of beef, *the brésil* and the pork-products were smoked. By manipulating it, using the cords and louvres located on the roof, it was possible to adjust the drawing and to smoke the pieces of meat, as required. It then remained only to leave them where they were, so that, due to the constant ventilation of the room, they retained their excellent quality throughout the year.

This *tué,* however, also had other uses: drying the hay, circulating air in winter, when other outlets were blocked by snow and ... shelter for swallows. Here also, cheeses were prepared.

LE COMTÉ

A thousand year tradition: the manufacture of cheeses in Franche-Comté is more than a thousand years old. It is said that the shepherds and herdsmen of "Séquanie" (Franche-Comté) themselves made very fine cheeses. At first, manufacturing these great cheeses was the only way in which milk could be preserved and food-stocks built up for the long, harsh winters of this region. In the 12th and 13th centuries, several "fructeries" produced large cheeses which enjoyed a great reputation. The large cheeses (fore-runners of the Comté gruyères) required a great deal of milk. So, the farmers joined forces and brought their produce to the "fructerie" or co-operative creamery. Today, almost 400 such creameries, faithful to this tradition, offer you each day, as in the Middle Ages, the opportunity to savour Comté gruyère. The word "gruyère" also takes its origin from the Middle Ages: the manufacture of cheeses required a lot of wood for heating the milk. The farmers traded with the "officiers gruyers". These officers, instituted by Charlemagne, managed the forests, which were called at that time, *grueries* (same derivation as *grume,* or "rough timber").

A designated area of quality milks: Faithful to their traditions, the manufacturers of Comté follow very specific regulations ratified by official order. Comté may only be manufactured in the Doubs, the Jura, Haute-Saône and a few other communes of the Ain, Saône-et-Loire and the Territoire-de-Belfort.

The manufacture of Comté requires top quality milks, supplied by cows of the Montbéliard and Pie rouge de l'Est breeds.

Their feed must be healthy and natural: mainly, grass and dry hay. Fermented feeds are strictly prohibited.

These 2 factors, designated produce area and high quality milk are the principal regulations concerning the manufacture of Comté. As a result, its production is deliberately restricted, consistent with tradition.

Its manufacture: Comté, a wheyey, moulded cheese, is still produced by craftsmen using untreated milk. The milk is taken once or twice a day to the dairy, and poured into vast vats, then to be heated to approximately 32°C and pressurized to make it curdle. After half an hour, the curds obtained are cut into tiny chips, the size of wheat grains. It is then slowly brought to a temperature of approximately 55°C, being stirred all the while to improve the flow of the whey. The master cheese-maker then removes the curds from the vat using a linen cloth, the imprint of which will remain on the rind of the Comté, and places it in a shaping mould. The mould is then subjected to pressure for a period of 24 hours.

The next day, the cheese is taken out of the mould and placed in a cool cellar for one month. During this period, the Comté is salted, rubbed and regularly turned. It is this salting which gives the rind of the Comté its colour and matures it.

WALK 1: SUGGESTED WALKS

Two day walks
1   From Metzeral to Markstein, 4 hours 20 minutes.
2   From Markstein to Thann, 6 hours 50 minutes.

Three day walks
1   From Wissembourg to Climbach, 2 hours 25 minutes.
2   From Climbach to Obersteinbach, 5 hours 40 minutes.
3   From Obersteinbach to Niederbronn-les-Bains, 4 hours 45 minutes.

Three day walks
1   From Ribeauvillé to Aubure, 3 hours.
2   From Aubure to the Tinfronce Refuge, 6 hours.
3   From the Tinfronce Refuge to Metzeral, 6 hours 25 minutes.

Three day walks
1   From Thann to the Belacker Farmhouse Inn, 3 hours 30 minutes.
2   From the Belacker Farmhouse Inn to the Ballon d'Alsace, 4 hours 25 minutes.
3   From the Ballon d'Alsace to Evette-Salbert, 5 hours 30 minutes.

Four day walks
1   From Schirmeck to Hohwald, 6 hours.
2   From Hohwald to Barr, 5 hours 15 minutes.
3   From Barr to Châtenois, 7 hours 45 minutes.
4   From Châtenois to Ribeauvillé, 4 hours 45 minutes.

Eleven day walks
1   From Schirmeck to Hohwald, 6 hours.
2   From Hohwald to Barr, 5 hours 15 minutes.
3   From Barr to Châtenois, 8 hours 30 minutes.
4   From Châtenois to Ribeauvillé, 4 hours 45 minutes.
5   From Ribeauvillé to the Col des Bagenelles, 6 hours 15 minutes.
6   From the Col des Bagenelles to the Tinfronce Refuge, 3 hours.
7   From the Tinfronce Refuge to Metzeral, 6 hours 15 minutes.
8   From Metzeral to the Grand Ballon Hotel, 6 hours 30 minutes.
9   From the Grand Ballon to Thann, 4 hours 45 minutes.
10 From Thann to the Ballon d'Alsace, 8 hours.
11 From the Ballon d'Alsace to Évette-Salbert., 5 hours 30 minutes.

Vallée du Doubs

WALK 1

WISSEMBOURG

⌂ 𝗔 ⚏ ✕ ▭ ⚙

(see map ref 1)
160m
12th to 14th century abbey
church of Saint-Pierre et
Saint-Paul, the 13th century
church of Saint-Jean;
Renaissance hôtel de ville,
old houses, ramparts.

The Stanislas old people's
home is the Petit Palais
where the King of Poland,
Stanislas Leszczinski, lived
from 1724 to 1725 after he
was dethroned. His daughter
Marie left there to become
Queen of France.

Detour 5 hrs 30 mins
Lauterbourg

1:30

Detour see left. You can reach Wissembourg from Lauterbourg via Scheibenhard and the Hardt Forest by taking the footpath of the Lignes de la Lauter. This is a line of fortifications built in 1706. This path is marked by a red white and red rectangle and finishes at Wissembourg station where it joins the GR53. See map 1:50,000 Vosges du Nord.

Take the GR53 west from the station along the Avenue de la Gare as far as the roundabout. At the Stichaner monument, where there is a signpost, take the D77, the Vosges route, to the left towards Climbach. At the first bend after leaving the built up area, take the road leading to the telecommunications mast which then follows the ruins of the Wissembourg line, a line of fortifications dating from 1708. It leads to the D3. Take the path which goes alongside the road as far as the Scherhol forester's lodge at a height of 312 metres.

Opposite the nursery, take the Sentier Dietenbeck which winds steeply up to the Tour de Scherhol summit.

Tour de Scherhol
506m
Ruins of observation tower 1895-1944; this is open mountain hut with water obtainable from refuge on col.

0:10

Follow the path down to the west as far as the Col du Pigeonnier.

COL DU PIGEONNIER
⌂
432m
View over plain of Alsace and Palatinate.

0:45

From the col take a path westwards, then a track, below the D3. Join the D3 shortly before the Climbach cemetery.

CLIMBACH
⌂ ⚒ ✕
(see map ref 2)
345m
A small summer resort.

0:45

Take the forest road to the right from the crossroads in the centre of Climbach. 500 metres past the Boesch forester's lodge leave the road and turn right to the hamlet of Petit-Wingen.

PETIT-WINGEN
✕
225m

1:00

From the restaurant, take the forest road on the right. About 300 metres from the last house, where the forest road bends sharply to the left, continue straight on along a forest track by the Heimbach stream. After 1.5 kilometres cross the road and the stream and follow a track just past the Heimbach pools. Take the forest road again, past the Col du Schaufelshald to the Col du Litschhof.

Col du Litschhof
(see map ref 3)
325m
Detour *10 mins.*
LE GIMBELHOF
⌂ ✕
342m

0:55

Take the forest road from the col and climb up to the southwest as far as the hotel and restaurant. You can join the GR again either along a footpath marked with a white disc leading to the ruins of Hohenbourg, or by going directly to the ruins of Fleckenstein which can be seen to the west. This path is marked with a red white and red rectangle. From the Col du Litschhof the path climbs to the southwest then turns north west to the Col du Hohenbourg.

Col du Hohenbourg
(see map ref 4)
475m
Junction with the GR from Dahn in Germany.
Detour *15 mins*
Château Hohenbourg
Take a path to the east.

The GR leaves the col by the path down the western side of the Langenfels rock, past the Fleckenstein farm and continues on to the ruins of Fleckenstein.

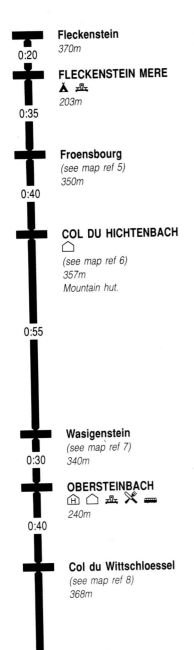

Fleckenstein
370m

0:20

FLECKENSTEIN MERE
203m

0:35

Froensbourg
(see map ref 5)
350m

0:40

COL DU HICHTENBACH
(see map ref 6)
357m
Mountain hut.

0:55

Wasigenstein
(see map ref 7)
340m

0:30

OBERSTEINBACH
240m

0:40

Col du Wittschloessel
(see map ref 8)
368m

Leave the castle, turn right down the Sauer valley to the Fleckenstein Mere.

Cross the stream flowing into the mere and take the path straight ahead down a steep slope for 500 metres. Take the path along the south side of Fuchsberg to the ruins of Froensbourg.

After the Château of Froensbourg continue west along a path and then a broad track for 100 metres. Take the gently sloping path on the right round the south spur of Falkenberg to the Col du Hichtenbach.

Take the path west from the col for about 600 metres, leading to another col at 398m. Climb up northwards taking care to follow the waymarking. 250 metres further on there is a crossroads. Take the track to the north east, then after about 400 metres take the path on the left which leads to the Zigeunerfels rock.

Continue along the same path as far as the D190 and follow it for 100 metres to the right as far as the Col du Wengelsbach at 383 metres. Take the track and then the path on the left leading down to the ruins of Wasigenstein.

Go down into the Langenbach valley on the path, cross the track and the stream. A path leads through meadows to Obersteinbach.

Cross the D3 southwards and then cross the Steinbach stream. Take the track on the right, then at the next fork the track on the left. In the forest, where several tracks cross, take the path up to the Col du Wittschloessel.

Cross a track and take the path to the left. At the first fork go down the path to the right leading to a forest track and follow it as far as the Col du Wineckerthal at a height of 334m. (Map ref 9).

On the col, cross a track and continue towards the south; go left at the next fork. (Map ref 10).

On the col, at 423m, take the path leading up

31

0:30

to the east with the mountain on the right; 250 metres further on turn sharply to the right then after another 150 metres turn left for the summit of Lindenkopf at 512m. Cross the plateau and then follow the path down the mountainside to the south west. (Map ref 11)

Turn sharply left then right; 400 metres further on take a track to the south. (Map ref 12).

At a col follow the track to the left to reach Windstein.

WINDSTEIN
🏠 🍷
(see map ref 13)

0:40

Go past the Inn and take the track leading immediately down to the right, then the path to the left which joins a track. When you leave the forest there is a sudden change of direction to the right towards the Gruenenthal valley at a height of 236m. Cross this valley.

Climb up along a forest track and at a fork take the path to the left which follows the edge of the forest and ends at the D53. Follow this road to the right as far as Wineckerthal.

WINECKERTHAL
🍷
222m

1:30

Take the road on the left and after 500 metres cross the D853. Go past the old Buchwald forester's lodge, and where the route forks follow the track towards the north west. (Map ref 14). Go along a path climbing up to the south west. This path crosses two forest tracks and after 1.5 kilometres reaches a track which you follow to the right. (Map ref 15). At the Col du Borneberg continue in the same direction. Shortly afterwards, near a forest hut, you reach the Grand Wintersberg road. Go up this road as far as the Col de la Liese.

COL DE LA LIESE
🍷
(see map ref 16)
514m
On rock behind tea chalet, there is a sculpture of a prehistoric divinity.

0:15

Take the path from the col which zigzags up to Grand Wintersberg.

Grand Wintersberg
581m
This is the highest point of the Northern Vosges. There is

From the summit take the path to the south. After several zigzags it crosses a forest track. A little further on take a track on the left which goes down to the Celtic Spring.

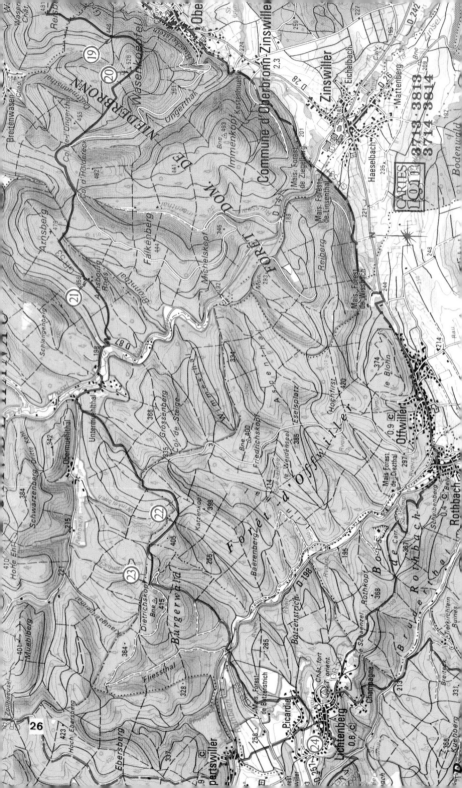

0:45

a belvedere 25 metres high built by the Club Vosgien in 1889. There is a view across the Vosges, the plain of Alsace, the Black Forest and the mountains of the nearby Palatinate.

The Celtic Spring

(see map ref 17)
This is also known as the Lichteneck Spring. It has exceptionally pure minerals and contains only 5mg of salts per litre. It is good for kidney and bladder infections.

0:25

Take the N62 southwards to Niederbronn-les-Bains.

NIEDERBRONN-LES-BAINS

195m

1:00

From the Hôtel de Ville Square cross the Falkenstein stream, go past the Protestant church on the left and the Hôtel des Postes on the right. Then turn to the right and follow the Rue de la Libération towards the station. Go past the English Garden. Before the station, opposite the hotel, turn to the left, cross under the railway track and go up the Allée des Tilleuls to the right. Pass under the new road bridge then take the path on the left which winds up through the King of Rome's Wood.

At the top, where you go into the National Forest, cross a track and take the path leading up the north east side of Reichsberg. Walk for about 20 minutes and follow a forest track for several metres. At the fork take the track on the left which climbs to the ruins of Wasenbourg.

Wasenbourg

(see map ref 18)
432m

0:30

Shortly after the ruins take a track on the right. 500 metres further on turn to the right, then at the next two forks take the left turn. A broad track leads to the Kreutztannen crossroads.

Kreutztannen crossroads

(see map ref 19)
448m

0:15

Take a track southwards, the track furthest to the right, then the first path on the right climbing up to Wasenkoepfel.

Wasenkoepfel

(see map ref 20)

0:25	*521m* *Belvedere Tower.*

Go down to the north west to the Col de l'Ungerthal.

Col de l'Ungerthal
439m

0:15

Follow the forest road north west to the Col du Holderheck.

Col du Holderheck
408m

Take the path to the west which climbs to Grand Arnsberg at a height of 465m.

0:30

Old boundary stones dating from 1764 marking frontier of the Lower Rhine and Moselle départements.

Take a path to the south west to the ruins of Grand-Arnsbourg.

Grand-Arnsbourg
(see map ref 21)
348m

0:25

The path goes down to the west and joins the D141. Turn right along this road towards Muhlthal

MUHLTHAL
✕
198m

In front of the restaurant, take a path to the left which crosses the Zinsel du Nord. Turn right and 500 metres further on take the Obermühltal road to the left. Shortly afterwards take the track on the left passing between two pools. Turn to the left then take the second path on the right. Don't climb up the steps. Follow this path up the mountainside on to the ridge. (Map ref 22).

2:15

Junction with the route from Offwiller waymarked with a vertical white line.

Follow this track to the west for about 700 metres. (Map ref 23). Take a path to the left leading down southwards into the Rothbach valley to Pulverbrucke at a height of 202m.

Cross the stream and the D198. Take the Lichtenberg road. Take the path immediately to your left which climbs up first through a forest then through meadows to the village of Lichtenberg

LICHTENBERG
⌂ △ ⚓ ✕
(see map ref 24)
320m
Detour *10 mins.*
Château de Lichtenberg
Twelfth century Château de Lichtenberg destroyed in 1260 by the Bishop of Metz and rebuilt in 1286 by Konrad de Lichtenberg,

In the village of Lichtenberg follow the D257 west for 250 metres. Turn left and before the transformer, take a path on the right which goes through fields to join the D157. Follow this road towards Wimmenau for about 350 metres. Take a path on the left which goes round Langrain to the south. Near the Kienberg forester's lodge take the D157 again to Wimmenau.

1:15

Bishop of Strasbourg. Besieged in 1677 by the French and conquered in 1678. Restored in 1680 and completely altered in the 19th century. After the Battle of Woerth in 1870, a detachment of German troops came and bombarded the fortress, and the small garrison was forced to surrender on August 10.

WIMMENAU

200m

This village was mentioned as long ago as the 9th century. Later it was part of the domain of the Lords of Lichtenberg. It was devastated during the Thirty Years War and later rebuilt by Swiss immigrants. There is an old church with a 12th century romanesque belfry.

1:40

Pass through the village starting from the station. Cross the bridge over the Moder and take the D919 to the right for 250 metres. Take a track to the left. At the first fork turn right and follow' the edge of the forest westwards and then southwards (Map ref 25). Cross a stream and go into the Petite-Pierre-Nord National Forest (Map ref 26). Go on to the Ochsenstall Rock. After leaving the forest you reach Erckartswiller.

ERCKARTSWILLER

(see map ref 27)
245m

1:20

Cross the village of Erckartswiller from east to west and take the D813 on the left. Cross over a bridge and take the dirt road on the right, then take a path on the left which goes to La Petite-Pierre.

LA PETITE-PIERRE

(see map ref 28)
340m
This is a national reserve for the conservation of deer. From the beginning of the 13th century the Counts of Lutzelstein, descendants of the Counts of Metz and Lunéville owned this land.

Junction with the GR532.
Detour *5 mins*
Château de la Petite-Pierre

From La Petite-Pierre go down to Kohlthalerhof via the Altenburg gardens, an old redoubt, and the Rocher du Corbeau. Take the D178 for 300 metres, then fork right towards the La Petite-Pierre mill pond nearby. Take the path on the right, going up towards Weyerkopf. Join the forest track at the La Petite-Pierre Eschbourg forester's lodge. Follow this track to the left for several metres then take the path on the right down into the Rehbach valley to the hamlet of Graufthal.

1:45

*North Vosges Regional
Nature Park Centre.*

GRAUFTHAL

0:45

(see map ref 29)
202m
*Famous for houses hewn out
of rock; ruins of Benedictine
convent founded in 8th
century by Bishop of Metz
can still be seen; the
convent, damaged during the
Peasants War in 1525, was
secularised in 1551.*

Junction with the GR 532.

Cross the village southwards. Turn to the right before the cemetery, cross the South Zinsel and follow a track to the left which goes along the Zinsel and joins the D133 (Map ref 30).

Fork from the GR532

The GR53 takes the D133 to the left to Oberhof.

OBERHOF

196m

Turn right at the crossroads in Oberhof. Cross the bridge, take a track on the right and straight after that the path leading up on the left to Fallberg. At the top the GR follows a forest track which joins the D122. Follow this road to the right for 1 kilometre (Map ref 31).

At La Colonne you reach the N4 and follow it to the right for 50 metres towards Phalsbourg. Take a forest track to the left and go behind the Kaltwiller forester's lodge (Map ref 32).

Cross the Pandours moat.

2:30

*Group of fortifications, moat
and ramparts which, from
prehistoric times, barred
route from the Col de
Saverne; during War of
Austrian Succession in 1744,
Pandours, Hungarians and
Croatians, under Colonel von
der Trenck, tried to stop
French troops from Lorraine
at this point.
(see map ref 33)*

Go on to the "Rocher du Saut du Prince Charles"

Rocher du Saut du Prince Charles
This is the most famous of the legendary rocks in the Saverne at an altitude of 370 metres. It is 15 metres high and overlooks an ancient Roman road. It also has a sacred grotto, a medieval place of pilgrimage. According to legend, a Duke of Lorraine called Charles, who was being pursued on horseback by his enemies, jumped from the top of the rock without hurting himself and continued his desperate ride. Steps lead to the top of the rock and the Col de Saverne Botanical Garden created in 1931 by the Saverne botanist Émile Walter.

SAVERNE

(see map ref 34)
190m
This town has geographical and strategic importance. Saverne is rich in historical monuments. The château was built by Cardinal Rohan in the 17th century, Napoleon III added two wings and it now houses the museum.

1:00

The Parish Church is 12th century; only the belfry porch is original. The nave was restored at the end of the 15th century. The Church of the Recollets was part of the convent built in 1303 by the Augustinian Monks of Obersteigen. There is a cloister in pure gothic style. The rose garden has more than 1300 varieties.

Haut-Barr
457m
12th century château. The plateau is dominated by three huge rocks 30m high with steps up from the courtyard. The southern one, called Markfels, marked the boundary of the Marmoutier

The GR goes past the monument to the writer Edmond. About, then on to Saverne.

Follow the Grand'rue de Saverne, cross the bridge over the Marne-Rhine Canal and take the towpath on the right at the Quay des Écoles. Before the first bridge go up some steps to the N4 and cross this road to the Rue du Haut-Barr. Further on you join the Haut-Barr road, the D171. Follow this road to the right then after the Hagondange Holiday Centre, take the forest track. A few metres further on take a fork on to a path leading to the Château of Haut-Barr.

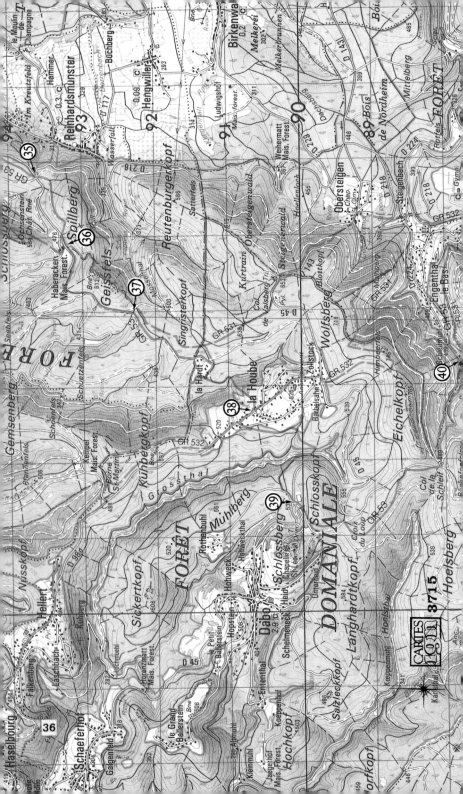

0:30

Abbey lands. The Pont du Diable, Devil's Bridge, links it to the central rock. Wonderful panoramic view from the top of these rocks. In the courtyard is a 12th century romanesque chapel, restored in 1880.

Originally installed in 1798 it was in use until 1852, and rebuilt in 1968.

When you leave the château take the road to the south, turn left after the car park and go past one of the 46 Chappe telegraph stations.

Go down the col past the fir tree planted to commemorate the centenary of the Club Vosgien, in 1972. At the foot of the châteaux called the Grand and Petit Geroldseck, the GR comes to the Table des Sorcières crossroads.

Table des Sorcières crossroads

0:30 *423m*

Go straight across and take a path opposite leading up to Brotschberg.

BROTSCHBERG

⌂

536m
Belvedere tower built in 1897 by Club Vosgien; extensive view all round; Mountain hut.

1:00

The path goes down to the south past a strangely shaped rock and the Brotsch cave. 1.5 kilometres further on pass the Schaeferplatz forester's lodge at a height of 382m.

Follow the forest road south for about 200 metres then take a path on the right parallel to the road leading to the Billebaum crossroads.

Billebaum crossroads.
(see map ref 35)
471m
There is a beech tree here about 350 years old with circumference of 5.75m.

0:30

Go straight across and take a path on the left going west, parallel to the road. You join the road again at Haberacker.

Haberacker
(see map ref 36)
485m
A few metres further on, below the road is a dilapidated forester's lodge.
Detour *20 mins*
via GR531
Rocher du Geissfels
0:45 *617m*
View point

Detour see left. Take the road south west from the crossroads. 200 metres further on take a path to the left, waymarked with a blue rectangle, leading to the Rocher du Geissfels. From the rock you can rejoin the GR53. Go towards a pylon and down a path to the south west (Map ref 37). Go past Geissfelswasen and join the GR53 again near it.

The GR53 leaves the road to the forester's lodge (Map ref 36) on the right and continues on the other road. 500 metres further on take the path on the left to the west. After another 250 metres turn to the south (Map ref 37). The GR53 passes near the Geissfelswasen kiosk to the La Hardt clearing.

La Hardt
530m

0:30

Skirt round the clearing towards the south. The GR passes the Amis des Vosges de Saverne Tourist Club Refuge, then turns to the left and the south, and goes down into the upper valley of the Baerenbach, which it crosses. Climb up through pasture land to a road which you reach opposite the church in La Hoube.

LA HOUBE
🏠 ⛲ ✕
(see map ref 38)
561m
This is a hamlet in the parish of Dabo, the highest village of Moselle.
Junction with the GR532.

0:45

Follow the road to the right going north for about 150 metres and at Les Alisiers holiday centre take a path on the left leading down to the south. Cross the valley and climb up again in a north westerly direction. 500 metres further on the path turns to the left and the south west. It joins the D45 at La Pépinière.

D45
(see map ref 39)
536m
Detour *10 mins*
ROCHER DE DABO
🏠 ✕
560m
Cross the D45 and take the road which climbs up to the Chapelle Saint-Léon where there is a view point.
Detour *20 mins*
DABO
🏠 ⌂ ⛲ ✕

0:45

Cross the D45, leaving the road which goes to the Rocher de Dabo on your right and climb up by a motor road in a south westerly direction. Before reaching the Chat Noir Inn, where there is no accommodation, take the path on the left leading into the forest. After about 2.5 kilometres from the D45 you reach a tarmac forest road near a reservoir, with a spring nearby. Follow this road to the right and the south to the Col de la Schleif.

from here via Sandplatz, MF de Hengst Crossman, col de Naviou join 53 again

COL DE LA SCHLEIF
⌂
689m
Picnic area with benches and tables.

0:30

Go down a path to the east from the Col de la Schleif into Schleifthal and join the D224 at the Rosskopf Inn.

ROSSKOPF INN
✕
(see map ref 40)
450m

0:45

Cross the road and the Mossig stream below the inn and take the path on the mountainside leading to Haut-de-l'Escalier, overlooking the resort of Wangenbourg.

Junction with the GR531

WANGENBOURG
🏠 ⌂ ⚒ ✕ 🚃
(see map ref 41)
460m

1:15

Climb up the forest track to the south from Haut-de-l'Escalier. After about 1.2 kilometres take a path on the right past the Col du Schneeberg at 870m to the Schneeberg rock.

Schneeberg
(see map ref 42)
961m

1:00

Come down from the rock and follow a path to the right and the south leading down to the Nideck forester's lodge.

NIDECK
🍷
(see map ref 43)
600m
Junction with the GR531 and the GR532.

0:15

Take the D218 to the right. 400 metres further on take a path to the left leading down to the ruins of the Châteaux du Nideck.

Châteaux du Nideck
(see map ref 44)
550m
Built in 13th century on older foundations, they belonged to Bishop of Strasbourg, and were destroyed by fire in 1636.

1:15

Go down from the Châteaux du Nideck into the Hasel valley, past the Nideck waterfall (Map ref 45).

Near the Nideck hotel and restaurant take the D218 to the left. After about 500 metres take a track on the right, cross the Hasel stream, turn left and continue along by the Hasel (Map ref 46).

Go behind the Luttenback campsite where there is accommodation. Cross the Weinbaechel stream at the saw mill and continue along the Hasel to the first houses of Oberhaslach.

OBERHASLACH
🏠 ⚒ ✕
(see map ref 47)
290m
The town centre is 900m to the east.

0:45

The GR53 goes down the Rue du Klinz. On a hairpin bend at the bottom of the hill turn right and take the Rue du Mittenbach. After a few metres take the Rue Grempil to the left. Where the road forks, by the last houses, turn left and follow the road which goes round the Stiftwald to the east. Cross the Meisenwald to Urmatt.

URMATT
🏠 ⚒ ✕ 🚃
250m

2:20

Take the Rue de Molsheim from the mairie. At the first intersection keep to the left, at the second go to the right and at the third climb up to the left. Turn right into the forest on the bend. The path leads down to the Eimmerbaechel valley. Further on, you see the old Kappelbronn forester's lodge below you. Then the GR zigzags up to La Porte de Pierre.

La Porte de Pierre
(see map ref 48)
858m
Oddly shaped rock which looks like a gate with several openings.
Detour *15 mins.*

0:30 **Le Petit Katzenberg**
903m
Flat rock fissured by erosion; a beautiful view.
Follow the path waymarked with a yellow triangle.

Rocher de Mutzig
1,010m

1:15

La Baraque Carrée
(see map ref 49)
0:30 *736m*

Col d l'Engin
(see map ref 50)
789m
0:45 *Junction with the GR5 from Abreschviller to the north west.*

Donon
1,009m
View point, orientation table. Donon was an important Celtic cultural centre. Many Gallo-Roman remains have been found here. Temples, bas-reliefs, sculptures etc. The most important ones are in the musuems at Épinal and Strasbourg.

0:45

DONON PLATFORM
🏠 ✗
(see map ref 51)
732m
Detour *5 mins*
Donon Hotel and
2:00 **Restaurant**
Take the D392 to the south west for 300 metres.

After La Porte de Pierre the GR follows a forest track which goes first to the west then to the north and then south to the Rocher de Mutzig.

The GR53 then continues to the Col du Narion at 924 metres, to Narion at 999 metres.On to the Le Noll clearing and then down to La Baraque Carrée.

After a Baraque Carrée the GR53 follows a mountain path below the ridge to the Col de l'Engin.

Follow the GR5 south. Pass the col Entre-les-Deux-Donons, at 823m, where there is a mountain hut belonging to the Club Vosgien. Then climb to the summit of Donon.

Go down from the summit to the south west, past the Pierre des Druides, a rock with potholes, to the left of the path. The D993 and the D392 cross at the Donon platform.

At the crossroads take the D392 towards Schirmeck to the south east. 350 metres further on turn right on the second path going down into the valley (Map ref 52). You come to a stream. The GR53 and the GR5 go up to the D392 and follow it to the right as it descends. 200 metres further on take a path on the left on the hillside. Pass above the village of Wackenbach where there is a café and

provisions. The GR53 and the GR5 join the D392 which you follow to the left as far as Schirmeck.

SCHIRMECK
🏠 ⛺ ⚒ ✕ 🚂
(see map ref 53)
315m
The GR53 ends at Schirmeck.

1:30

By the Schirmeck Hôtel de Ville take the path leading up by the side of the château, which is a reconstruction of a small medieval castle. Go past the Barembach cross at 416m and the Leopold Fountain to the former Struthof camp.

Struthof
(see map ref 54)
699m
Struthof is unfortunately well known for the extermination camp set up by the Germans in 1941-1944. There were more than 30,000 victims. There is a monument, a national cemetery and a museum.
Junction with the GR532.

1:00

The GR5 passes below the Struthof camp, near the memorial. It joins the D130 then follows this road to the south. Below the road to the right you can see the former Arbeitslager, the concentration camp during the Nazi occupation. Leave the road at the Col de Chenagoutte at 850m and take a track on the left to the east north east (Map ref 55). Near a harnesssed stream at 908m take a path to the right which goes first to the east and then to the south east. Pass by a mountain gîte to the Champ du Messin.

Champ du Messin
(see map ref 56)
1,031m
The Bechstein Fountain is named after the General Secretary of the Club Vosgien from 1893 to 1918.

0:20

Follow the D130 for about 600 metres. On a left bend in the road take a forest track on the right leading to the Col de la Katzmatt.

Col de la Katzmatt
(see map ref 57)
1,018m

0:30

The GR takes a sharp bend to the right towards the south west to the Rocher de Rathsamhausen.

Rocher de Rathsamhausen
1,025m
View point.

1:00

Junction with the G531

From this rock, the GR joins a Roman road and follows it to the south south west. Cross the D214 to the Vieille Métairie (Map ref 58).

The GRs join the D214 at the Col du Champ de Feu.

Col du Champ de Feu
(see map ref 59)
1,075m
Fork from the GR531.
Detour *10 mins.*
Champ de Feu Tower

On the Col du Champ de Feu take the path below the one on which you arrived, at a sharp angle to the north east. After about 1 kilometre, near the Andlau spring, go diagonally to the east. Cross three forest roads to the Hohwald waterfall (Map ref 60). Take the path to the left

The Club Vosgien
This club was founded in Saverne in 1872 by Richard Stieve. The Club has a constitution drawn up in accordance with the local Civil Code. It was recognised as a public service by the decree of 30th December, 1879. The aim of the Club is the development of walking and outdoor activities in the Vosges, the Alsace Jura, the Alsace Plain and the Lorraine Plateau. To this end the Club researches, establishes, waymarks and maintains public footpaths, view points and historic sites. The Club also builds, establishes and runs refuges, camping grounds and mountain huts. The Club edits guides, maps and other literary or artistic works which publicise the region from a geographical, historical or scientific point of view. The Club studies the means and takes the necessary initiatives to protect the natural environment in these regions.

The group has 30,000 members divided into 90 local sections and organised by a central committee. Its special objective is to open the Vosges to tourists and make these mountains better known.
PAUL KELLER.

1:45

The tower was built in 1898 to commemorate the 25th anniversary of the founding of the Club Vosgien. A magnificient view point. Take the road to the south.

in a north easterly direction past the commemorative stone of the Grand Sapin de Strasbourg. Further on you come to the health resort of Hohwald.

HOHWALD
🏠 ⌂ Å ☎ ✕
750m

0:45

From Hohwald take the D426 towards Mont-Sainte-Odile. At the first bend to the right after the church, take the path on the left going north east and climb up through the forest to the Welschbruch forester's lodge.

WELSCHBRUCH FORESTER'S LODGE.
🍷 ✕
780m

The GR continues to the north east parallel to the D426 below it (Map ref 61).

To the south of the Breitmatt crossroads cut across the D426. On the southern slope of Kienberg the GR reaches the crossroads of the D426 and the D854, also called the Bloss crossroads (Map ref 62).

2:00

Cross this junction and climb up some steps to the path to the north, which passes the Pagan Wall and the Beckenfels.

You come to the convent of Mont-Sainte-Odile.

CONVENT OF MONT-SAINTE-ODILE
🍷 ✕

When you leave the Convent of Mont-Sainte-Odile, go down the steps immediately to the left, then follow the Way of the Cross to the

(see map ref 63)
764m
A first rate cultural and
religious centre.
Detour *5 hrs*

0:30

Circuit of the Pagan Wall.
Waymarked by a yellow
bracket.
The Pagan Wall is one of the
most important prehistoric
monuments in Europe and
probably dates from 8th
century BC; rebuilt by the
Romans in the 4th century.

Maennelstein
817m
Remarkable view point over
Rhine Plain, the Black Forest
and Vosges; orientation table.

0:45

Château du Landsberg
580m

1:15

BARR
🏛 ⌂ ♨ 🍷 ✕ 🚋
200m
Renaissance style hôtel de
ville built in 1640; Protestant
church has romanesque and
gothic belfry.

1:00

ANDLAU
🏛 ♨ ✕ 🚋
240m
Abbey church here, built in
the 11th, 17th and 18th
centuries and some old
houses.

1:00

GRUCKERT
⌂
(see map ref 65)
580m

right. At the second fork keep to the left and cross the Plateau de la Bloss at 823m and go down to the Maennelstein sign.

Follow the path along the south slope of La Bloss to the west as far as Schaftstein and then on to Wachstein at 760m (Map ref 64).

Outside the Pagan Wall go down left to the south as far as the Jadelot kiosk, a view point. Then continue on to the ruins of the Château du Landsberg.

Continue on down, past the little kiosk at a height of 462m, and the Moenkalb forester's lodge at 410m, then past the Héring monument. The GR goes on to Barr through the Kirchberg vineyard.

Leave Barr by the Route du Vin towards Mittelbergheim. At the crossroads before the cemetery take the track on the right which crosses the vineyard and leads to Andlau.

Cross Andlau from south west to north west. Past the church take the Rue Clémenceau and after about 400 metres, take the Gruckert track going up on the left to join the Weihermattenthal track. Take this track, to the left, in a south westerly direction. You arrive at the old Gruckert forester's lodge.

At the Gruckert forester's lodge the GR5 follows the track which passes behind the annexe and leads up to the south south west via Hasselbach at 630m. After about 30

minutes you reach the Col de l'Ungersberg at 675m. Continue on another 150 metres from the col in the same direction (Map ref 66). Take the first track on the left in a south easterly direction. It soon turns to the south. About 1 kilometre from the col cross a forest track. The path leads up opposite and joins another forest track. Turn left along this track, then take a path on the right which zigzags up to the foot of the Ungersberg tower.

1:15

Ungersberg
901m
View point with small
observation platform.

Descend from the summit towards the south to a small col at 751m. Here take the forest track to the east which skirts round Baerenberg, 765m. After about 500 metres take a path on the left, turning north, which joins a forest track. Follow this track to the right and to the south (Map ref 67).

At a crossroads at a height of 437m the GR follows the road and leaves it, to turn right, 100 metres further on. Then it turns to the left past summits with an altitude of 476 and 451m (Map ref 68).

2:15

Just before reaching the road, at a height of 392m, turn right towards the Neumatten farm. From here follow the road to the left as far as the crossroads at 357m, and go straight across. Continue on to Schulwaldplatz at 490m then to the Kaesmarkt crossroads and the Bernstein ruins.

Bernstein ruins.
(see map ref 69)
562m
Ancient fortress destroyed
during Thirty Years War;
pentagonal keep and a
knights' hall with romanesque
windows.

The GR follows a road to the south leading to the Ortenberg ruins.

1:00

Ortenberg ruins.
490m
Ancient 13th century fortress
with walls 17m high in almost
white granite, surmounted by
a strong pentagonal keep,
37m high.

Leave the old fortress in a south westerly direction. The path goes down past Ramstein, another fortress, to Huehnelmuehle.

0:30

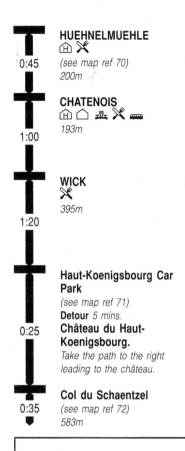

HUEHNELMUEHLE
(see map ref 70)
200m

Follow the road east. At the intersection with the D35, the Route du Vin, turn south to Châtenois.

CHATENOIS
193m

Cross the level crossing. Take the N59 on the right for 400 metres, towards Sainte-Marie-aux-Mines. Take the Rue du Hahnenberg on the left. Turn right past the forester's lodge to the old forester's lodge in Wick.

WICK
395m

Continue to the south then take a path parallel to the D159, which you cross twice. After crossing it for the second time take the path on the left passing behind the Haut-Koenigsbourg Hotel. The GR joins the road to the Haut-Koenigsbourg Car Park.

Haut-Koenigsbourg Car Park
(see map ref 71)
Detour *5 mins.*
Château du Haut-Koenigsbourg.
Take the path to the right leading to the château.

The GR follows the path to the west as far as the Col du Schaentzel.

Col du Schaentzel
(see map ref 72)
583m

Take the D42 towards Thannenkirch. 80 metres further on the GR goes to the right on a forest path leading to Thannenkirch.

The Château du Haut-Koenigsbourg
The Château du Haut-Koenigsbourg is the only fortress in Alsace which has been rebuilt.

According to a document of Charlemagne's of 774, the mountain it is built on was called Stephansberg. In 1147 it appears as Castrum Estufin. In 1192 as Kungesberg, royal mountain. The name Château du Haut-Koeningsberg is at variance with Château de Kintzheim (Koenigsheim). In the 13th century the Duke of Lorraine, who owned it, gave it as a fief to the Counts of Werd, Landgraves of Lower Alsace. In the 15th century it had become the lair of robber barons and Haut-Koenigsbourg was besieged, taken and destroyed in 1462 by contingents from the town. In 1479 the emperor gave it to the Swiss counts of Thierstein who restored it in lavish style. In 1633 it was besieged and destroyed by the Swedes. It was bought by the town of Sélestat in 1865. In 1899 Sélestat presented it to the German emperor, William II, who had it refurbished under the direction of the architect Bodo Ebhardt. There is much discussion about its restoration, but its appearance is altogether imposing. There is a paid guided tour.

THANNENKIRCH
ⓗ ⚒ ✗

510m
Detour *3 hrs*
**The Quatre-Chênes
crossroads.**

0:35

From the centre of Thannenkirch follow path 4c
leading up to the Taennchel Ridge. On the
plateau follow path 8a to the north then 1c
(Map ref A). At the Roche des Trois Tables,
take path 8a by Langfelsen, the Pagan Wall
(Map ref B). Go on to the Rocher de la Paix
d'Udine (Map ref C). Cross the Hasenclever
crossroads then the Cerisier Noir crossroads
(Map ref 73). At the Quatre-Chênes crossroads
join the GR5 again. From the south end of the
village the GR continues south on a small
stony road. It takes a path to the right by a
bench and goes into the forest. It joins a forest
track. After 800 metres, cross a stream and
continue upwards (Map ref 73). The GR goes
on to the Quatres-Chênes crossroads then to
the Château de Haut-Ribeaupierre.

Château de Haut-Ribeaupierre
650m
*Highest of the three châteaux
of Ribeauvillé; keep can be
visited and offers good view
of the region.*

0:15

Go down to the south to the Château de Saint-
Ulrich.

Château de Saint-Ulrich
510m
*Major reinforcement work
going on; best preserved
château; keep can be
visited; view over Ribeauvillé
and Strengbach valley.*
Detour *5 mins*
Château du Guirsberg
*On a steep rock to the east
of the Château de Saint-
Ulrich.*

0:35

From the Château de Saint-Ulrich go down the
path to the right, twice crossing the ancient
wall round the outbuildings of the château. A
little lower down, the path goes along past
some impressive rocks and continues down
through vineyards. It comes out on the Place
de la République in Ribeauvillé.

RIBEAUVILLÉ
ⓗ ⚐ ⚒ ✗ ▭

(see map ref 74)
265m
Town of the strolling fiddlers.

1:25

Follow the street west for 170 metres. Go past
a wayside crucifix and cross the bridge over
the Strengbach. Follow the road to the left for
220 metres.

Take the Rue Saint-Morand to the right. The
path passes between some houses then enters
a forest, firstly among chestnut trees, then
beeches and pines, coming out at the Col du
Seelacker.

The Vineyards of Alsace

Alsace is one of the most northerly wine growing provinces of France. Its vineyards cover the hills below the Vosges mountains, from north to south, over a length of about 100 km. The vineyards are sheltered from the cold winds and exposed to the sun. The limestone ground retains the heat so that the vine is not easily affected by late spring frosts. Alsace wine matures excellently thanks to the warm dry autumns of the province's semi-continental climate. Alsace produces excellent white wines, graded according to the type of grape. These are the high class grapes: the Sylvaner, Tokay, Riesling, Muscat d'Alsace, Gewürtztraminer. There is only one vin rosé, the Pinot noir.

Alsace wine is a cheerful and spirited companion. To raise the spirits, serve a Muscat as an aperitif, or failing that an exquisite fruity Riesling. With seafood serve a Sylvaner, a Pinot or a light Riesling. Drink a Riesling with fish cooked au bleu or in sauce or grilled. It has a delicate bouquet which complements the lightness of the fish. Take a light wine, a Sylvaner or better still a strong Riesling, with sauerkraut, a rich Tokay with Strasbourg foie gras or game, and a Gewürtztraminer with Munster cheese, this can be served with the dessert as well.

Col du Seelacker
673m

Climb up to the west then to the north to arrive at a crossroads (Map ref 75).

Detour *10 mins*
Bilstein ruins
Ancient fortress with access to keep; view over Strengbach valley and châteaux of Ribeauvillé.

0:45

Continue to the west past an iron crucifix, Flodererkreuz, to the Rocher du Koenigsstuhl.

Rocher du Koenigsstuhl
938m
This rock is shaped like a throne, hence its name.

0:50

The path follows the ridge and goes on to the Rocher du Tétras.

View point.

Shortly afterwards it leaves the ridge to the right and descends to Aubure.

AUBURE
(see map ref 76)
800m
Highest mountain village in Alsace, with very small population; health resort which has been converted to a convalescence centre; relaxing holiday centre with various tourist attractions.

1:15

From the crossroads in the centre follow the road to the Col de Fréland for 700 metres. At this Col take the road towards the Salem Spa. 800 metres further on climb up to the right on the track leading to the Trois-Bans stone.

TROIS-BANS STONE
⌂
(see map ref 77)
1,128m
*Boundary of Aubure, Fréland
and Sainte-Marie-aux-Mines,
Club Vosgien mountain hut.
Junction with the GR532*

1:00

Fork from the GR532.

The GR continues to the west then the south west on the southern slope of Rehberg (Map ref 78).

The GR5 goes on to Petit Brézouard at 1,206m, and shortly afterwards, past a mountain hut, to Grand Brézouard.

Grand Brézouard
1,228m
*This is the highest granite
massif in the Vosges to the
north of the Kaysersberg
valley. There is a panoramic
view: to the west, Saint-Dié
and the mountains bordering
the Moselle valley; to the
north the Champ du Feu and
the two Donons; to the south
the mountains of the upper
Moselle.*

0:15

The path goes down first to the south and shortly afterwards directly north to a col.

Col
(see map ref 79)
1,090m
*This is situated between
Rauenthal and Le
Bonhomme.*

0:45

Follow the path to the west past a rustic wooden chalet. Cross a forest track to reach the Col des Bagenelles.

COL DES BAGENELLES
⌂
903m

0:35

The path descends to the south, near the road, to the village of Le Bonhomme.

LE BONHOMME
🏠 ⚒ ✕
(see map ref 80)
690m
Junction with the GR532.

0:40

Leave the village by the little path to the south opposite the church, and climb up through fields to join a road. Take this road to the left, to the south east, and follow it past some houses and into the forest. In the wood the road turns right then left, past the *gîte d'étape* at the Devin Mere.

THE DEVIN MERE
⌂ 🐾
(see map ref 81)
950m

The GR passes near the remains of German construction work dating from the 1914-1918 War, then reaches the Devin Mere at a height of 929m.

0:40

This Mere is surrounded by rocky doline; today there is only a marsh; interesting flora conservation area; explanatory notice board.

Take a path to the left of the mere, twisting up through woods to the Roche du Corbeau.

The Roche du Corbeau
1,130m
Here you can still see major construction work undertaken by the Germans during the First World War. Before reaching the rock you pass the upper station of the funicular railway from Lapoutroie, which offers shelter. It was linked to the building at the summit of the Tête des Faux by a tunnel 1,100m long, which has now collapsed. The Roche du Corbeau is a fine view point.

Go to the west then take the small path on the right and climb up to the Tête des Faux.

0:25

Tête des Faux
1,220m
The summit consists of an impressive pile of rocks and the remains of German military fortifications. There is a fine panorama. In 1914-1915 this summit was the scene of heavy fighting. The French and German positions were very close. The group of fortifications of the Tête des Faux was unique of its kind on the western front from 1914-1918.

Descend from the summit, first across scree to the south west, and then to the south as far as the Duchesne crossroads.

0:15

The Duchesne crossroads
(see map ref 82)
1,125m
Junction with the GR532.

Take a forest track which skirts the two Têtes des Immerlins on the west, to the Tinfronce Refuge.

0:25

TINFRONCE REFUGE
⌂ ✗
1,110m
tel

The GR5 continues to the south to the Calvary Col of Lake Blanc.

0:10

COL DU CALVAIRE DU LAC BLANC

(see map ref 83)
1,144m
300m to the east is the Blancrupt Refuge where you can find lodging and meals, and a hotel.
Junction with the GR531 and GR532.

Extensive views.

0:55

Gazon du Faing
(see map ref 84)
1,302m
Detour *5 mins.*
GAZON DU FAING INN

Take the track marked "Plainfaing" and descend to the west from the orientation table, as far as the ridge route.

1:10

Roche du Tanet
1,293m

1:00

COL DE LA SCHLUCHT
(see map ref 85)
1,139m
Rescue Post
About 20 minutes from the

Continue towards Lake Blanc on the D48 for about 200 metres. Past the Longwy holiday centre, which is below the road, take a track to the right towards the west, past the centre, then take a path and climb up to Reichsberg (part of the High-Haulms), a long ridge above Lake Blanc, on the old frontier between France and Germany.

About 800 metres from the holiday centre, at a fork, you can either climb up to the right to the ridge, or take the path to the left which follows the cornice above Lake Blanc. There is a magnificent view of the lake and the Alsace plain.

By a spring, turn to the right and the west, then 200 metres further on, to the left and the south.

The GR follows the old frontier, now the departmental boundary, as far as the orientation table at the Gazon du Faing.

The GR5 continues, sometimes climbing, sometimes descending, at an altitude between 1200 and 1300m, towards the Col de la Schlucht. Pass above the Lake des Truites (or Forlet) to the Gazon de Faîte at 1301m, to reach a col at 1228m just beside the D61 above Lake Vert or Soultzeren. The GR climbs up again to the Roche du Tanet.

The GR passes by other impressive rocks, (Wurtzelstein or Haut-Fourneau; later, on the Alsace side, are Hirschsteine and Spitzenfels) before reaching the Col de la Schlucht.

Alternative route 2hrs 30mins to Schaeferthal (Map ref 87). Opposite the café des Roches, take the path, Sentier des Roches, waymarked by a blue rectangle. See the dotted line on the map.

Col de la Schlucht, below the road going from la Schlucht to Hohneck, is the Chalet des Amis de la Nature. 300 metres from the GR, south of the Col de la Schlucht, is the Schlucht University Chalet. The Col de la Schlucht is the highest, and most frequented route of the southern Vosges. It is on the border between the Départements of Haut-Rhin and Vosges. Junction with the GR531.

1:00

From the Col de la Schlucht, the GR5 climbs up through the forest, still southwards, to the Col du Falimont. Pass close by the Trois-Fours Farmhouse Inn, and the Trois-Fours Refuge which belongs to the CAF. Go along the steep rock wall which descends to the bleak cirque of Frankenthal. This takes you to Le Hohneck.

Finest group of rocks in this wall, is Martinswand, which offers some fine climbing, but only for experienced climbers; dangerous.

LE HOHNECK

(see map ref 86)
1,362m
Extensive panoramic view; orientation table.

Alternative route along the ridge. This is waymarked by a red rectangle with a white stripe. From Le Hohneck you can reach the Col du Herrenberg without going down into the valley. A lovely path, along the ridge all the way, leads to the Col du Herrenberg. This path crosses Kastelberg, at an altitude of 1,345m, passes by the Firstmiss (or Ferschmuss) Farmhouse Inn and the Rainkopf Refuge Chalet which belongs to the Mulhouse section of the Club Vosgien. From there it climbs up to Rainkopf at 1,304m, passes Rothenbachkopf, at 1,315m, and Batteriekopf at 1,310m to reach the Col du Herrenberg.

2:30

Le Hohneck

The GR5 descends from the Hohneck summit to the east as far as the Col du Schaeferthal, then continues down along the south flank of Petit Hohneck, near the Schiessroth Farmhouse Inn. Just before the inn go down the winding path through the forest, as far as Lake Schiessrothried; meals and limited accommodation are available; open from the 15th May to the 15th October.

0:50

LAKE SCHIESSROTHRIED

(see map ref 88)
920m
Rescue post with limited accommodation, not permanently manned; Strasbourg la Vogésia Gym Club Holiday Centre; Colmar

Cross the dyke and take the path to the left leading down to Lake Fischboedle.

0:15

*Vosges Trotters Touring Club
Refuge Chalet.
A series of jagged granite
rock faces making up the
Spitzkoepfe chain surround
the lake.
Junction with the GR521.*

Lake Fischboedle
*(see map ref 89)
790m
One of Vosges most
picturesque lakes; on the
right is a large moraine
dating from ice age.*

1:00

METZERAL
*(see map ref 91)
480m
Largest village of "Big
Valley" of Fecht; almost
entirely destroyed during
First World War.*

0:45

MITTLACH
*(see map ref 92)
530m
Village founded in 18th
century by Catholic
woodcutters from Tyrol.*

1:50

Col du Herrenberg
*(see map ref 93)
1,186m
Splendid view of upper Thur
valley and mountain tops
along its southern edge;
nearby, below Ridge Route,
is Hus Farmhouse Inn and
Mulhouse Ski Club Refuge.*

1:00

The path continues down through the valley of the Wormsa, with its scree covered slopes.

Alternative route (Map ref 90). When you leave the Wormsa valley a forest track leads directly to Mittlach avoiding Metzeral. This shortens the walk by 4.5 kilometres, that is about an hour's walking. This route is waymarked with a red rectangle like the GR5.

The GR5 crosses the river Fecht and reaches Metzeral.

From the Place de la Mairie in Metzeral, take the D10 to the west as far as Mittlach.

Take the valley road to the south of the village. At the next left bend in the road, after the Renaud forester's lodge, continue straight along the path up into the forest. Then, 150 metres further on, climb up to the left by the waymarked path. A few zigzags through the forest, up the slopes of the Herrenberg, lead to a forest track. The GR passes by the ruins of the old Herrenberg farm to reach the ridge at the Col du Herrenberg.

The GR5 continues to the south along the west slope of the ridge and the Ridge Route to the Col du Hahnenbrunnen.

**COL DU
HAHNENBRUNNEN**

⌂

1,190m

0:50 *About 250 metres south
below ridge is
Hahnenbrunnen guest house.*

MARKSTEIN

⌂ ✕

(see map ref 94)
1,200m
Large tourist centre.

*This route through the haulms
offers a fine view towards the
valley of Saint-Amarin and
the Rossberg-Drumont-Grand
Ventron Ridge.*

*The etymology of this place
name is disputed. The first
name makes reference to the
Hungarian assassination, in
1:20 925, of 7 monks of the
Abbey of Murbach who had
fled the invaders. The
second is an allusion to the
damp nature of the area.*

*Nearby is Florival de
Guebwiller Ski Club Refuge;
further on is path marked
with a yellow rectangle and if
you follow Grand Ballon
direction, you reach
Riedisheim Ski Club Refuge;
near same path marked with
yellow rectangle, but in
Hundskopf-Markstein
direction, is Mulhouse Sports
Union Refuge.*

⌂

Col du Haag

♉ ✕

1,231m

0:30

The path continues towards Breitfirst at 1283m,
crosses the D27 and then the Ridge Route at
an altitude of 1208m. The GR goes along the
east flank of Trehkopf and Jungfrauenkopf, to
reach the tourist resort of Markstein.

The GR crosses the Ridge Route towards the
Grand Ballon, and goes along the south west
slope of Marksteinkopf, at an altitude of 1241m.

3 kilometres further on you reach the pasture
land of Mordfeld or Moorfeld.

Alternative route across the Ridge Route
(Map ref 95). You can follow the path
waymarked with a red rectangle striped with
white, which climbs to the summit of
Storkenkopf. There is a fine view.

The GR5 goes round Storkenkopf to the south.
At an altitude of 1366m it is the second highest
summit in the Vosges. A little below, halfway
between Mordfeld and Haag, is a mountain hut
which is always open. The GR reaches the Col
du Haag.

The GR then climbs up the south slope to the
summit of the Grand Ballon.

Grand Ballon
1,424m
Highest point of Vosges.

0:15

**HOTEL DU GRAND-
BALLON**
🏠 ✕
(see map ref 96)

0:40

**Du Ballon Farmhouse
Inn**
1,110m

0:20

Col du Firstacker
940m
*Chapel commemorating
Sudel summit (1,011m)
battles of First World War.*

0:30

Col Amic
(see map ref 97)
825m

0:15

Château du Freundstein
928m
*10 minutes south is
Freundstein Farmhouse Inn.
This little fortress perched on
a rock, was the highest of
the Vosges châteaux. There
was just one tower which
was inhabited. Its few
remains were ruined further
in the First World War, when
it served as a look-out post
for the French Artillery.*

0:35

Go past the Blue Devils Monument. It commemorates the sacrifice of the Chasseur Battalions during the 1914-1918 War. Then go to the orientation table where there is an all-round panorama over the Vosges, the Alsace plain, the Black Forest and in clear weather, the Alps, visible from Santis to Mont Blanc. The closest area of the Alps, the Bernese Oberland, with the Jungfrau and the Eiger, is only 180km away.

Go down from the summit to the north east as far as the Hôtel du Grand-Ballon.

Follow the road south for about 300 metres. Near a ski lift take the path to the left, which goes down through haulms to the Du Ballon Farmhouse Inn.

Cross the Ridge Route, go down through the pasture land cutting off a large bend in the road. Cross the road a second time and then go into the forest. The path leads to the Col du Firstacker.

After the Firstacker clearing the GR keeps within the forest, a little way from the Ridge Route, and reaches the Col Amic.

The GR goes across the crossroads and down into the forest below the road to reach the Château du Freundstein.

The GR goes to the south east and reaches the Col du Silberloch.

COL DU SILBERLOCH
900m
Name recalls old silver mine;
the whole area as far as
Thann is rich in thin veins of
metal which were worked in
the past.
Detour *30 mins.*
Hartmannswillerkopf
956m
Summit, marked with tall
cross, offers wonderful view.

Below the summit is a
farmhouse with
accommodation at 1,040m.

Molkenrain Refuge
(see map ref 98)
1,094m

Turenne's Camp
During Great War, important
staging post on French
military route towards Vieil
Armand sector, from
Bitschwiller.

Château de
l'Engelsbourg
(see map ref 99)
445m
13th century ruined fortress;
when it was demolished by
Turenne's troops in 1674,
they blew up cylindrical
keep; one section fell without
breaking and was called
"The Witch's Eye"; beautiful
view over Thann and
Thanner Hubel.

THANN
(see map ref 100)

0:40

0:25

1:30

0:15

From Silberloch take the path opposite the restaurant which climbs towards Molkenrain.

The GR climbs up through the haulms at the top leaving the actual summit on the right and passes close to the Molkenrain Refuge.

The GR goes down to Turenne's Camp.

The GR continues to descend, keeping to the west flank of Glaserberg then Baecherkopf and reaches the Pyramids Camp, another wartime staging post. It goes round past Ertzenbachkopf and reaches the Col du Grumbach at 580m. Then it continues along the Rosenbourg to the Château de l'Engelsbourg.

The GR goes down through the valley of Kattenbach to Thann.

Go along by the Place de la République, over the level crossing, take the Rue Kléber and then immediately to the right, the Rue des Jardins, and to the right again the Staufen

0:25

This is a beautiful old town, famous for its well-proportioned Collegiate Church of Saint-Thiébaut, in very pure 14th-15th century gothic style. As soon as you reach the bridge over the Thur, you will notice the Witches' Tower, one of the last traces of the medieval fortifications. There is an interesting local museum.

track, and follow it as far as the Col du Staufen.

Col du Staufen
(see map ref 101)
474m

0:45

The path climbs up through woods, passing the Place du Roi de Rome at 560m, then close to the "Guata Brunne", meaning "Good Fountain", and a strange oak tree with six trunks.Then it reaches the Diebolt-Scherer Level.

Diebolt-Scherer Level
⌂
625m

0:25

From there the GR follows a precipitous route passing the Devil's Rock (Teufelskanzel), with a view over the impressive Thanner Hubel, and rejoins the Col du Hundsruecken.

COL DU HUNDSRUECKEN
✗
748m
Highest point of Joffre Route, built by French troops during First World War, to link Doller Valley (Masevaux) to Thur Valley.

The GR climbs through a thick fir tree plantation, as far as the Haut-de-Bourbach, at 871m.

THANNER HUBEL
⌂
(see map ref 102)

1:05

Alternative route Thanner Hubel. You can follow the path marked with the red triangle, leading to the Thanner-Hubel farm which has a dormitory.

A little further on is the Thann-Vosges Ski Club Refuge. A path going off to the left leads to the summit of Thanner Hubel, at 1,182m, which offers one of the finest views in the Vosges. Rejoin the GR5 at the Col du Rossberg (Map ref 103).

At a place called Haut de Bourbach, at 871m, the GR5 goes north west through the forest and comes out on the haulms near the Col du Rossberg.

COL DU ROSSBERG
⌂
(see map ref 103)
1,100m

0:30

Vogelsteine Rocks
(see map ref 104)
1,180m
Also called Falkensteine, or
"falcons' rocks".
Junction with the GR 532.

0:20

BELACKER FARMHOUSE INN
✉ ✕ 🛏
(see map ref 105)
979m
Fork from the GR532.

1:25

Lac des Perches Col
(see map ref 106)
1,070m
Detour *30 mins*
Via GR531
ROUGE GAZON HAULM
⌂ ⌂ ✕ 🛏
1,090m
Follow the path waymarked
with a blue rectangle, to the
north.

0:50

Col des Charbonniers
(see map ref 107)
1,117m
Detour *30 mins*
LE GRESSON-MOYEN
⌂ ✕
Follow the path waymarked
with a blue triangle.

Pass the Rossberg Farmhouse Inn, a little below, to the north, 400 metres to your right. A little further on pass the Mulhouse Ski Club Refuge. Walk over haulms to reach the rocks called Vogelsteine.

From the top of the Vogelsteine, go down to the north west as far as the Belacker Farmhouse Inn.

The GR then continues on an exposed path along the southern flank of Stiptkopf, passes on to the Col du Rimbach, then enters the forest and stays within it nearly all the way to the Col des Charbonniers. It passes a very short distance from the summit of Johanneskopf, at 999m, then to Rimbachkopf at 1,194m. You can either go round this summit or climb it. Descend steeply towards the Lac des Perches Col.

From the Lac des Perches Col, also known as Sternseesattel, the GR5 goes along the steep rock wall of Tête des Perches, height 1,222m. 100 metres from the col on the path over a boulder field, at 985m, there is a splendid view of the lake. This name, like the lake's, also called Sternsee, is a corruption of the place name "Bers". The GR goes through woods to reach the Haute-Bers pastures, where there are ruins of the old farm. After a good look at the lovely Gresson pastures and the Wissgrut-Baerenkopf Ridge, which forms the southern slope of the Doller valley, enter the forest again. A little further on there is a splendid view over the two Neuweiher Lakes at 820m, and you reach the Col des Charbonniers.

After the Col des Charbonniers, the GR follows the ridge. Forest paths and open spaces alternate. Here and there are outcrops of rocks and carpets of heather. This section is just like a balcony over the distant Masevaux valley. You can see Lake Alfeld below. About 30 minutes from the Col des Charbonniers, you will see a path on the right.

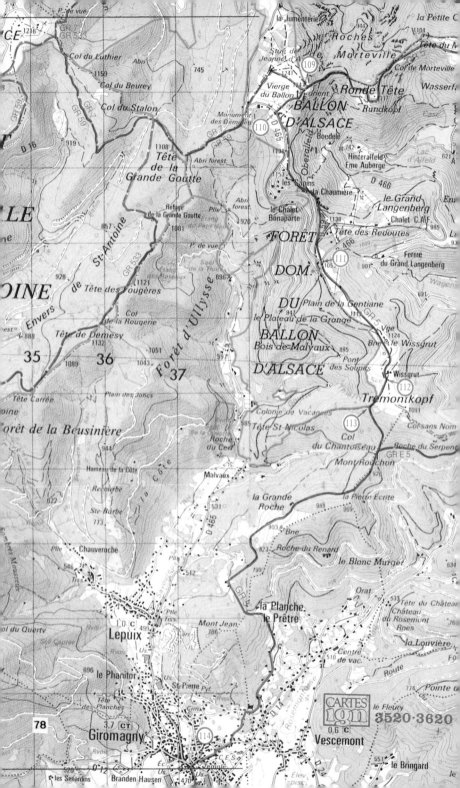

Detour *10 mins*
(see map ref 108)
La Petite-Chaume
Mountain Hut
This is on the slope beyond
the ridge looking towards the
Charbonniers Valley.

2:10

Named after miners of
German and Swedish origin
who, towards the end of the
16th century, were
encouraged to settle by the
Duke of Lorraine, to work
iron and copper mines.
Mining stopped in 1761 and
the miners turned to making
charcoal.

Climbing to summit of Ballon
d'Alsace is difficult; before
snow melts, impracticable.

BALLON D'ALSACE
(see map ref 109)
1,247m
The most southerly of Vosges
summits over 1,200m, spans
Haut-Rhin, Vosges and
Territoire de Belfort
départements; its vast

0:10

flattened crown provides
splendid view over large part
of Vosges, Trouée de Belfort
and Alps; orientation table.
Junction with the GR7 and
the GR59 which have a joint
route to the west as far as
the Col du Luthier.

BALLON D'ALSACE
FARM
(see map ref 110)
1,170m
Detour *2 hours*
SAINT-MAURICE-SUR-
MOSELLE
550m

The GR passes on to Ronde Tête, or Rundkopf. You come to the foot of the steep rock which forms the eastern slope of the Ballon d'Alsace. It is hollowed out in a deep cirque falling in several stages as far as lake Alfed.

At the far end of the summit plateau, there is an equestrian statue of Joan of Arc, a patriotic symbol put up in 1909, close to the Franco-German frontier of the time. The GR7 and the GR59 pass by there.

From the orientation table the GR5 goes towards the statue of the Virgin, and comes down as far as the Ballon d'Alsace farm.

Go down to the north from the Ballon d'Alsace, to the Jumenterie, then follow the path waymarked with a red disc.

Detour *1 hr 45 mins*
SEWEN
🏠 🚉 ✕ 🚌
0:40
501m

Follow the path waymarked with a red rectangle and a white stripe, first to the south and then along the Langenberg. The GR follows the D465 towards the south, from the Ballon d'Alsace farm. 300 metres further on, take a path on the left which climbs gently before going down along a ski piste.

Beautiful view over the lake and the Trou de la Chaudière glacial cirque.

Go along beside the road, following a path overhanging this road, to reach the Col du Plain de la Gentiane.

Col du Plain de la Gentiane
(see map ref 111)
0:30
1,055m

Cross the road, go below Wissgrut and climb up a broad track as far as the Wissgrut farm.

Wissgrut Farm
(see map ref 112)
1,080m
Now uninhabited.
Detour *2 hrs 20 mins*
MASEVAUX
🏠 🚉 ✕ 🚌
450m
Follow the path waymarked with a red rectangle which passes by Fennematt, a farmhouse inn, then
2:00
Baerenkopf at 1,074m and Sudel, 915m.
(see map ref 113)
View point over the Savoureuse valley.

100 metres to the south take a path on the right which descends gently through pasture land, and skirts the wood. At a place called the Gros Hêtre, enter the wood and turn to the left. After a steep descent in the forest, you reach the Col du Chantoiseau at 918m. Go straight on avoiding the forest road; the path climbs very steeply then descends very regularly.

The route passes beside the Grande Roche, leaves the cover of the forest and goes down regularly. It is then flat as far as the Col du Mont Jean. Turn left to the east here on a path which goes off to the south by the first houses. Follow a small road which quickly descends to the D14 and reaches the centre of Giromagny.

GIROMAGNY
🏠 ⌂ 🚉 🍷 ✕
(see map ref 114)
470m

In Giromagny go through the suburb of Belfort to the south. 250 metres further on take the Rue des Prés-Hayd on the right, then the Rue Sous-la-Côte on the left. Then go towards the forest. In the wood turn left in a southerly direction. After the sportsground cross a small road, continuing directly south, then join a track and follow it to the right. Go between some pools to reach an old military road and follow this to the left and the south as far as

1:20

Giromagny

Giromagny is a very old town. It was first mentioned in 1347. The town owes its development to the working of silver, copper and lead mines in the 16th and 17th centuries. The Comté of Rosemont was linked to France by the Treaty of Westphalia in 1648, and the mines were given by Louis XIV to Cardinal Mazarin. The stately home built in 1517 and called the "Maison Mazarin", dominates the main square. In the centre of the town a fountain, built in 1758, bears a Latin inscription. It refers to the union of the Comté of Rosemont with Alsace.

Since the crisis in the textile industry, the craftsmen and sub-contracting firms, mainly servicing the Belfort-Montbéliard industrial area, have revitalised this small industrial town beneath the Vosges. Thanks to its privileged position at the foot of the Vosges, Giromagny is the departure point for many walks into the Ballon d'Alsace Massif.

the D13. Follow this road to the left for 150 metres, then go to the right to reach La Chapelle-sous-Chaux.

LA CHAPELLE-SOUS-CHAUX
△ ⓨ ✕ ▥
416m

At the stop sign near the church, take the road to the right, go along the river and then cross it. The track rises and soon gives you a broad view over a region which is dotted with pools. In the background is Belfort and the Salbert Massif.

1:00

At the end of the street follow the track to the south which goes along by pasture land for 100 metres. At another crossing take the route due south. After crossing a wooded area, pass between two pools. Take the road which goes along the lake, as far as Evette-Salbert.

EVETTE-SALBERT
⌂ ⋏ ⚓ ⓨ ✕ ▥ ⚒
(see map ref 115)
397m
Junction with the GR533.
Fork from the GR533.
(see map ref 116)

Cross the railway track and take the road to the left, then go left again on the Rue du Val, which becomes a dirt road. Cross a bridge, and 600 metres further on you reach a fork.

0:30

The GR5 turns to the right on a track leading to Salbert.

SALBERT
⚓
437m

Take the D24 to the left then the D8 to the right, and 100 metres further on, leave it for a path leading up through a wood. You come out on an esplanade, surrounded by fortifications, Fort Salbert.

0:30

Fort Salbert
(see map ref 117)

The GR goes down to cross the Haute-Saône canal then crosses the N19 into Chalonvillars.

625m
5 mins west of GR is Fort
summit at 647m.
Vast panorama of Belfort,
1:00 *Pays de Montbéliard,*
southern Vosges, Black
Forest, Jura and Alps; 3
orientation tables.
Detour *30 mins*
BELFORT

Belfort, City of the Lion

In feudal times, Belfort, perched on the rock, was only a little town protected by its château. It was not until the end of the 17th century, that Vauban gave it the appearance we see today. Making a new start, the Sun King's Marshall created what today we would call a new town. The streets were gauged for carriages, the Place d'Armes was designed for troop movements, the houses built to specified designs, and protected by high octagonal walls.

There were two monumental gates for access. La Porte de France, destroyed in 1892, was on the present Place de la République. The Porte de Brisach, which has been recently restored, looks on either side, much as it was in Vauban's times. The impressive view from the Cité des Associations over the whole of the Citadel and its north east front, gives some idea of the the size of the fortifications undertaken by Vauban.

Inside the walls, apart from the old world charm of narrow streets, such as Étuve, Canon d'Or, and Diable, the Hôtel de Ville built in 1724 for the Noblat family and bought by the townspeople of Belfort in 1784 is worth seeing.

So are the cathedral of Saint-Christophe, opened for worship in 1750, with a fine organ of the period, built by Valtrin; and towers 27, 41 and 46 are essential parts of the fortifications' defence system.

The view westwards from the small Arsenal over the Lion and the Fortress is impressive. One may then go to the Lion's Terrace before climbing the postern path into the château. Here are moats, underground passages and galleries to be visited. The historical museum in the château has many collections tracing 65 centuries of history of the region. A few paces from there is a Museum of Art in a "Haxo Battery". The Bourgeois Tower has recently been restored, and there is access by the curtain path.

Why is it called the Belfort *"territory"*?

Until 1870 Belfort was part of the département of Haut-Rhin in Alsace. During the war of 1870 - 1871, the entrenched Belfort Camp, under the command of Denfert Rochereau, resisted a 103 day siege by the Prussian armies without yielding. This heroic resistance sealed the destiny of the town. The negotiators of the Treaty of Versailles kept Belfort in its French "administrative district", whilst Alsace and Lorraine were annexed to Prussia. Up to 1922 Belfort and the 106 parishes in its territory were still called Haut-Rhin. On 11th March 1922, the Belfort territory became the 90th French département.

CHALONVILLARS
🏨 🍷 🍴 🚉
390m

At the centre of the village take the Chatebier road to the right, then 50 metres further on take the track to the left which leads up to the church and joins a small road. Follow this as far as the edge of the wood then take the track on the left to join the D218. Take this road to the right, then 300 metres further on take the forest track on the left. At the intersection the GR follows the track to the right then a path which climbs gradually up to the left with a view over Chagey and its massif. After going through woods for more than 1.5 kilometres, you join a broad track. Follow this track to the left as far as Echenans.

1:30

View over Belfort.
(see map ref 118)

ECHENANS
🚉
380m

When you reach the D130, take the small road to the left and then to the right, through a housing estate. Cross a stream then enter the wood. At the first bend take the path to the right round a large meadow. It cuts across a strategic route.

(see map ref 119)
Junction with a PR leading to Héricourt.

0:45

50 metres further on take a good track which goes towards the south east along a pasture land fence. When you leave the wood pass between two cultivated fields and then climb up along a clump of trees. You arrive at some isolated houses. Descend by a road as far as the N83 and cross it. The GR crosses the Strasbourg-Lyon railway line and enters Brévilliers.

BRÉVILLIERS
🚉 🍷 🚉
(see map ref 120)
357m
Junction with a PR leading to Héricourt, where there is a railway station.
30 mins.
Detour *20 mins*
Dolmen de Brévilliers
The earliest research goes back to 1924, since when several excavations have discovered different objects, such as arrowheads,

Detour see left. The dolmen of Brévilliers, which is known by the old people in the village as "Pierre des Gaulois" "The Gauls' Stone", lies to the south east of the built up area in the Bois des Issières. Arrows mark the route from the village.

fragments of vases, stones used as weapons, bones.... This communal burial place dates from the Bronze Age, 2000-1800 BC.

1:40

(see map ref 121) 18th century frontier posts, on the border of Montbéliard and France.

CHATENOIS-LES-FORGES

🏠 ⛼ 🍷 🍴 🚌

(see map ref 122)
340m

0:25

NOMMAY

⛼ 🍷 🚌

330m

1:25

FESCHES-LE-CHATEL

🏠 🍴 🍷 ⛼ 🚌

(see map ref 123)
330m

Cross the village of Brévilliers from north to south. At the crossroads take a small road on the left, then 100 metres further on, take a track on the left going up through meadows, with a view over the new towns of Montbéliard and the Jura. You pass the South European oil pipeline. Immediately after entering the wood, take the path on the left.

After a long stretch through the wood, join the Châtenois road and follow it to the east. Enter the town near a transformer, take a road on the right and then immediately afterwards a path which goes through meadows, to reach the Vrai Bois track. Go along Rue Kléber and then Rue de Villars to reach a sandstone cross which is 300 metres from the centre of Châtenois-les-Forges.

Near the cross take a road on the right which has extensive views over the Savoureuse valley and the Jura, and leads to Nommay.

Cross the N437, go along the street opposite for 50 metres, then go off to the left northwards, to get back on to the D424. Continue as far as the bridge and turn to the right just afterwards. Go down the Sablière track. A broad track goes between the Savoureuse river and some old gravel pits which provided material for the motorway. They have since been converted into fishing lakes. Before a high tension pylon turn to the left, pass between two gravel pits and go as far as the motorway. Go along beside it for 300 metres. Take the D278 to cross the A36. Just before the canal bridge take the towpath on the right and follow it for 2 kilometres to the Rhône-Rhine canal. Use the lock to cross the canal. Another towpath to the right leads to a bridge, then turn left to reach Fesches-le-Châtel.

WALK 2

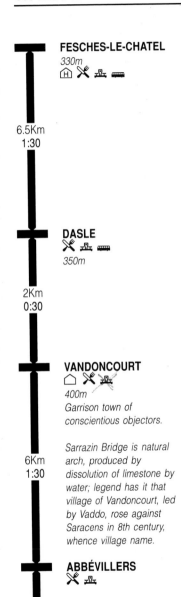

FESCHES-LE-CHATEL
330m

6.5Km
1:30

DASLE
350m

2Km
0:30

VANDONCOURT
400m
*Garrison town of
conscientious objectors.*

*Sarrazin Bridge is natural
arch, produced by
dissolution of limestone by
water; legend has it that
village of Vandoncourt, led
by Vaddo, rose against
Saracens in 8th century,
whence village name.*

6Km
1:30

ABBÉVILLERS

The GR leaves the lower village by a tarmac road situated to the right of the chapel; it skirts the cemetery to the left and arrives at the edge of the forest (benches and tables). It enters the wood as a straight walk bearing north east-south west and reaching an altitude of 402m; then, bear south and cross the N463 to enter the wood of Fahy; after walking to the end of a long, straight lane, skirt a vast felling area on the left, to rejoin the Étupes to Dasles road. Follow this westwards; 500 metres further on, turn left and into the forest by a footpath which leads directly to Dasle.

Cross the village taking the first road on the right; cut across the Dasle-Beaucourt road, continuing opposite along a road crossing the Champs de la Velle to reach the cemetery of Vandoncourt. Here, you find the yellow and red markings of the Regional Montbéliard GR, leading west into the Doubs Valley. The GR turns left or east and 250 metres further on, to the right making for Vandoncourt.

Leaving the village, the GR takes the Sarrazin Bridge road and down into a small valley where there are kennels.

At the Sarrazin Bridge, the GR does not go under the natural arch, but 50 metres before, it climbs up a wooden stairway. It then follows an access road, skirts a vast clearing then reaches the edge of the wood at the Siblot combe. Then, take a gravel track heading for the Six Chemins crossroads and which leads to Abbévillers.

The GR crosses the village straight ahead on the Meslières road and, when it turns westwards (height 565m on the 1: 50,000 IGN map), take a road straight ahead bearing towards the hillside. Once past it, go down into the little valley bearing west, cross a stream then follow it for about 500 metres. You then

10Km
2:30

join a very steep road, which you take on the right alongside a private estate, then turn left to cross the alluvial plain and arrive at the "La Papeterie" café-restaurant, and here, bear left (east), and climb a path to the top of the valley to the Franco-Swiss frontier. Go sharp right (south) and follow the frontier, identified by large stone markers. The path is very clear and there is no danger of straying; 4 kilometres further on, leave the frontier at the point where it makes a right-angle (south), to come into open country and then into a large pasture where the path twists and turns, from which you emerge on to a development road leading to Villars-lès-Blamont.

VILLARS-LES-BLAMONT
✗ ♨

Cross Villars-lès-Blamont and take the road for Chamesol; 100 metres further on, at the first bend, take the path straight in front of you, which is a short cut; you will rejoin the road after 200 metres, follow it for 700 metres and, at the first hairpin bend, turn right into the forest following the path climbing towards the ridge. The GR crosses a rocky combe and, following the ridge, comes to the redoubt of the old Fort Lomont Battery.

Batterie du Fort du Lomont
Walkers should pay attention to waymarkings when crossing the forest.
Panorama of Montbéliard Region and Belfort Gap.

6Km
1:30

Cross the fortifications ditch, continuing along the strategic track up to the right of a large farm which can be seen below. At this point the GR leaves the track and bears left downhill towards the pastures. You reach a development track, where you turn right; you come across two cattle grids; 150 metres past the second grid, take the gravelled track on the left, which goes down to a road you take left towards Ferme le Tremblois.

Ferme Le Tremblois
You will find the yellow and red markings of the Regional Montbéliard GR which lead east then south to Soulce-Cernay, where the local GR meets the GR5 on the way to Saint-Hippolyte.

After the farm, the GR turns right on to a road leading to Chamesol.

CHAMESOL
✗ ♨
Detour *Clémont Chalet*

On leaving the village, take the D121E in the direction of Saint-Hippolyte; 1,500 metres further on, you join the D121 which you cross

See broken line on map.

■
4Km
1:00

Saint-Hippolyte
370m
*The GR does not lead into
the village, through which in
fact, the local Montbéliard
GR passes.*
Detour *15 mins*
SAINT-HIPPOLYTE
🏠 ⛺ ✕ ⚓ 🚃
*Continue to descend along
the road skirting the
cemetery to the south, skirt
the old SNCF station, cross
the Doubs and go into the
town.*

6Km
1:30

*The local GR follows the
same route as the GR5 as
far as Soulce.
The local Montbéliard GR
does not cross the Doubs,
but stays on the same bank
and climbs north up the
small road to the left.*

SOULCE-CERNAY
✕
390m

6Km
1:45

COURTEFONTAINE
⌂ ✕
770m

to continue opposite on a road bordered by
dry-stone walls and hedgerows. The GR goes
down into the Doubs Valley over a path
through a wood, then along a tarmac road. You
pass the Chapelle du Mont on the left and
reach the cemetery of Saint-Hippolyte.

Opposite the cemetery, take the road on the
left (D121), which shortly bends east on the
edge of the plateau. Below, a little further on,
you glimpse the hamlet of Seignes, and
discover on the right side of the road that the
GR has just assumed the yellow and red
markings of the Montbéliard Regional GR,
coming from Saint-Hippolyte. The GR5 and
local GR continue along the dirt track. You go
on to the abandoned farm of La Grosse Roche.
Immediately after this, turn right on to a track
descending to the ruined Roche windmill, then
carry on as far as the hamlet of La Saunerie
and you come alongside the Doubs. The GR5
crosses the bridge over the Doubs and enters
the village of Soulce-Cernay.

After crossing the bridge, turn left then right on
to the first track, climbing to the D134 which
you take, left; 500 metres further on, leaving
the bend, turn left on to a wooded track joining
the D134 again. Follow this left for 250 metres.
On the bend, take a track left into young fir-
trees; 125 metres further on, before a meadow,
bear right on a sunken path climbing to the
Lajoux Farm. Continue along a track through
meadows as far as the Race Farm; take the
tarmac road which leads you to the village of
Courtefontaine, 2 kilometres away.

Behind the Courtefontaine church take a street
to the right, cut across the D134 to continue
opposite, and 80 metres further on turn left on
to a track joining the D134; follow it right for

7Km
1:45

500 metres; then turn right into a track across some fields. You cut across a road and reach the la Mine farms. At the last building, still going south, follow a track into some fir trees; soon, you pass an access road to a farm on the right; then continue on the edge of the fir plantation up to the Le Creux Farm. After that, turn left or east to go in to the trees, passing a number of paths on right and left, and 300 metres further on, turn left or north. As you leave the fir plantation, bear right until you reach a building named "La Girode". Continue along the track for approximately 250 metres; here, pass the access road to the Montassiers-Dessus Farm on the right, and turn left into the meadow. The track, at first clearly visible, then peters out; continue towards a spinney and go through it; you come out at the Montassiers-Dessous Farm. Here, take the slowly descending road right; 1,200 metres further on, when the road turns left, turn right onto a grassy track climbing to the village of Fessevillers.

FESSEVILLERS
△ ✕

861m

Leaving the village, the track climbs southward towards the Briquez farms, then to buildings in the *Sur le Mont de Fessevillers* locality.

Sur le Mont de Fessevillers

1,020m

6Km
1:30

Between the Sur le Mont de Fessevillers locality and le Bief d'Étoz, the old GR5 route passing through Urtière and Charmauvillers has been abandoned, as it contained too many tarmac roads.

Here, in the Sur le Mont de Fessevillers area, the GR5 bears east along a path beside a wood. You come out into a wide pasture: then, take a new forest track hewn in the rock, on the hillside. The GR reaches the Montbaron road which you leave soon after, to descend left to the D437B road (former N437B). Take this road right (south); 300 metres further on, descend on the left as far as the village of Goumois.

GOUMOIS
△ ⌂ ⋀ ✕ ⚓

From here, the GR5 skirts the left bank of the Doubs as far as Bief d'Etoz.

6Km
1:30

Along the Doubs gorges, the "Société des sentiers du Doubs" has established a network of paths, waymarked in black on limestone slabs, providing access for walkers to many wonderful beauty spots.

BIEF D'ÉTOZ ✗

At the Chapel of Bief d'Étoz, the GR5 continues along the left bank of the Doubs; 3 kilometres further on, you reach a junction with other paths, from which either of two routes can be taken to reach the Refrain electrics factory: the alternative route along the Doubs, avoiding the Échelles de la Mort, is indicated on the map by a dotted line; or by the GR5 which takes the Échelles de la Mort. In spite of their forbidding name, these ladders present no problem as they are a metal staircase and a hand rail. Then, at the junction of the paths, the GR5 leaves the bottom of the gorges to

7Km
1:45

Detour *1 hr*
VAUDEY
⌂

Detour *30 mins*
BOIS DE LA BICHE
🏠 ✕

take a right turn on to a path, climbing through woods on the Glassworks Hill. You will pass by the ruins of the Charbonnière Farm. Further on, you will pass a path on the right.

Detour see left. By bearing right and upward along this path, you can arrive at Vaudey.

Detour *30 mins*
CHEZ RENAUD
⌂ ✕

The GR5 arrives at the Echelles de la Mort passage.

The GR5 goes ~~up~~ *down* the ladders, then down into the scree to the Refrain electrics factory.

Échelles de la Mort
Three metal ladders, one after the other, enabling you to negotiate an overhang and descend into the valley of the Doubs.

3Km
1:00

Junction with the alternative route coming from the Bief d'Étoz by the edges of the Doubs. At the electrics factory, the GR5 takes the road right; 2 kilometres further on, before a hairpin bend, take the Refrain dam road left.

Le Refrain Dam

Skirt the stretch of water, climb a metal ladder and pass a path right climbing to Fournet-Blancheroche. Continue along the stretch of water; after the ruins of the Gaillots Farm, climb to the N464 which you take left; 300 metres further on, turn right on to a path dominating the Doubs. You cross a rocky spur, then by following a stony path you reach the locality of La Rasse.

4Km
1:00

LA RASSE
⌂ ⌂ ✕ ▭

Cross the Doubs and take the road right on the Swiss bank.

Detour *15 mins*
MAISON-MONSIEUR
⌂

3Km
0:45

The GR5 continues along the Doubs where there should be no camping, due to danger from floods, as far as the Bonaparte Path junction.

Bonaparte Path
617m
Indicated by an entry sign.

Here, there are two routes the walker can take to reach the village of Le Pissoux, either by the GR5 route by the Doubs gorges, or by the alternative route by the plateau (described below). After the Bonaparte Path junction, the GR5 follows the Doubs gorges along a clear and unmistakeably waymarked path, as far as the Chatelot Dam, passes in front of the electrics factory 3 kilometres downstream of the dam on the Swiss side and comes out at the Chatelot Dam.

8Km
2:00

Bonaparte Path

Alternative route by the Plateau. The alternative route climbs through woods by the Bonaparte Path onto the plateau, where it crosses fencing and bears left towards a farm.

107

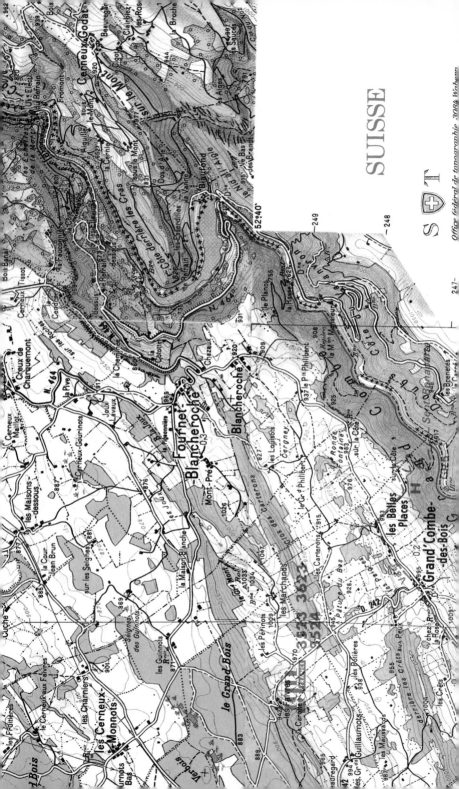

SUISSE

S ⊕ T

Office fédéral de topographie 3084 Wabern

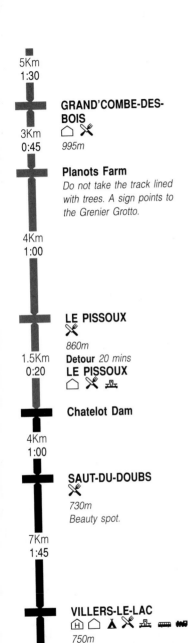

5Km
1:30

GRAND'COMBE-DES-BOIS ⌂ ✕

3Km
0:45   *995m*

Planots Farm
Do not take the track lined with trees. A sign points to the Grenier Grotto.

4Km
1:00

LE PISSOUX ✕
860m
Detour *20 mins*

1.5Km   **LE PISSOUX** ⌂ ✕ 🏛
0:20

Chatelot Dam

4Km
1:00

SAUT-DU-DOUBS ✕
730m
Beauty spot.

7Km
1:45

VILLERS-LE-LAC 🏠 ⌂ ⋏ ✕ 🏛 🚌 🚣
750m
Important clock and watchmaking centre; crossing point to Switzerland.

3Km
0:45

Take the farm access road to reach the hamlet of Belles Places. Then turn left on to a road leading to Grand'Combe-des-Bois.

Leave the village by the road heading towards Bardoux; follow it as far as a junction at 999m at Ferme des Planots.

The GR passes behind the farm and enters the Manchot wood. By a grassy shelf, go down bearing left where you see a sign on a rock and an arrow and by a very winding path, go past the view point of the Grenier Grotto, the Chapeau de Gendarme and to the foot of the Grenier Grotto. The path continues on the hillside as far as the Chez Némorin Farm; here, take the forest track south climbing to the village of Le Pissoux.

From the village of Le Pissoux, the alternative route takes the road descending to the Chatelot Dam.

The GR5 crosses the Chatelot Dam esplanade and descends metal stairs. The path then skirts the stretch of water called Lake Moron as far as Saut-du-Doubs.

At the first view point, take a path downwards in the direction of the waterfall (you can also go to a second lookout point situated 100 metres to the left); you pass by souvenir shops, a restaurant and the landing stage of the Villers-le-Lac boat. Climb right along a stony path to the new road which you take as far as Vions; then, still by the road dominating the Doubs basins you reach Villers-le-Lac.

Cross the Doubs; approximately 100 metres further on, take the station road right. Past the level crossing, turn right onto a gravelled track climbing to the "Côte Grillon" then by a tarmac road, you reach the Fermes de Prélot.

Saut-du-Doubs

If a person were unaware that the Doubs would once again meet the tumultuous passage through the gorges, he would conjure up the picture, unique to Switzerland, of a preserved fjord where the water remains immobilized by its reflections or the ices of winter. Here, the Doubs culminates in awesome plenitude; it proceeds only slowly and as if mysteriously gathering itself in before the waterfall.

However, the air is already filled with a distant murmur. Everything seems to harken towards it, and a fine spray rises from the chasm into which the Doubs dashes itself with such great élan. A waterfall twenty-seven metres high - the pure whiteness of atomized water, host to rainbows and myriad scintillations - makes up the kaleidoscopic extravaganza of the Saut-du-Doubs, which fades into black, swirling, steaming waters.

LOUIS LOZE

Fermes de Prélot
Detour *CAF refuge*

Continue on the road in a south easterly direction as far as the hamlet of Chaffaud.

2Km
0:40

Lookout point of Creuseys following ridge left.

SUR LA ROCHE

1,140m

5Km
1:20

LE GROS GARDOT

1,090m

4Km
1:00

At the Prélot farms, the GR5 turns right on to a track leading towards Gradoz and you come out on to a tarmac road which you take, left, as far as a transformer. Here, turn right into a pasture and climb onto the "Creuseys" ridge.

Cross a pasture and proceed to the Chopard farm; you will be in the Sur la Roche area.

The GR5 bears right on a track; 200 metres further on, opposite the second Chopard farm, turn left, through a gate, cross a pasture and climb up along a path through undergrowth on to the frontier ridge, the "Haut des Roussottes" locality (at 1,188 m). Here, turn right; the GR climbs a little further and will follow close to the skyline for approximately 3 kilometres. You come out on to a new road which you will have to follow to cross the Petit-Gardot pasture, then by a good track you will reach Le Gros Gardot.

The GR takes the D48 heading for Montlebon; after a few hundred metres, it turns left to the west towards Les Feuves. It crosses a vast clearing over a good track, passes a hamlet to the south, forks right or north, then left or north-west over a road which crosses a wood. It passes between hay meadows on a plot boundary to the locality of Vion-Billard, then reaches the overhang at the rear of Le Mont. Skirt this overhang, bearing south through

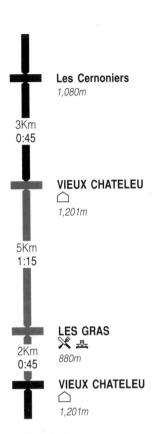

Les Cernoniers
1,080m

3Km
0:45

VIEUX CHATELEU
⌂
1,201m

5Km
1:15

LES GRAS
✕ 🪑
2Km
0:45
880m

VIEUX CHATELEU
⌂
1,201m

enclosed areas, then climb again by a road leading to Les Cernoniers.

The GR leaves Les Cernoniers by the tarmac road, to take a track right with a gate across it, which you go over. Do not turn into the wood, but to the right to the middle of the pastures. You follow a long combe to arrive at a newly opened road climbing to the Vieux Chateleu Farm.

Shortly after the farm, you can take two possible routes: the hilly alternative route by Les Gras, or the GR5, which reaches Le Grand-Mont directly.

Alternative route by Les Gras. This route is indicated on the map by a broken line.

By the summit of Les Ages, Le Meix Bosson and Le Rozet, you reach Les Gras.

Bearing south south west, the alternative route reaches Le Grand-Mont

After the Vieux-Chateleu farm, the GR5 takes the track bearing west climbing to Chateleu; 300 metres further on, turn left on to a track

Vallée du Doubs

5Km
1:15

GRAND MONT
⌂
1,034m
Junction with alternative route
coming from Vieux Chateleu.

2Km
0:30

Le Théverot
900m

7Km
2:00

descending to the bottom of the valley. Follow a small stream to the road, which you take south west as far as Nid du Fol. Here, turn left, then, at the next crossroads, take the road right heading for Les Gras; 100 metres further on, near a drinking trough, turn left into a pasture, go down the valley and into the forest. By a track leading south west you reach the hamlet of Les Seignes. Here, bear right towards the village of Grand Mont.

Near the former Grand Mont school, the GR5 turns on to a track which descends to the hamlet of Le Théverot.

Here, there are two routes you can take to Les Alliés.

Alternative route by Montbenoît. By a farmhouse, a little before the Théverot one, past a small bridge on the left, turn right into the middle of the pastures; go into the woods, climb the hillside of the Roches du Cerf, and you reach the ridge. Continue opposite into a pasture to cut across the D47. At the corner of a shed, take a path climbing to a small ridge where there is a TV booster, then descend through some woods as far as a clearing, which you skirt bearing right. You go on to the ruins of Lomont at 999m. From here, you cross a felling area; the forest track turns left but do not leave the "Grand Bois". Go on to some very tall pines, cut across a tarmac road at 940m and by a gravelled lane, you reach a crossroads at 936m. Turn left here, and a little further on to the right in the middle of a fir plantation. When you leave the fir-trees, you come out on to a vast plateau which you cross by following the marks on fence pickets as far as the hamlet of Le Mont de Spey. Turn right on to the road and 80 metres further on, left on to a path descending the hillside, first into pastures, then into fir plantations; you cross the Doubs over a footbridge and arrive by a sawmill yard at Montbenoît.

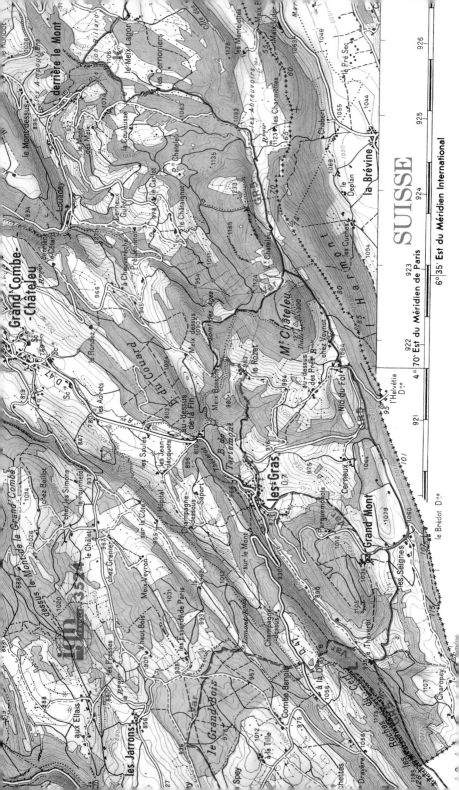

MONTBENOIT
⌂ ⌂ ⚡ ✕ ⚒ ▭ ◼
780m

The GR leaves the town by the N437 in the direction of Pontarlier; 1 kilometre further on, it crosses the Doubs and takes the Hauterive-la-Fresse road, then, on a bend, turns left or south to reach a small road; turn left here in the direction of Hauterive-la-Fresse.

HAUTERIVE-LA-FRESSE
⌂

Follow the Doubs Valley to Maisons-du-Bois.

11Km
2:45

MAISONS-DU-BOIS
⌂ ✕

Maisons-du-Bois is situated on the far bank of the Doubs. It is here that the GR595, which leads to Besançon via the Loue Valley, makes an appearance (see Topoguide 590-595).

The GR5 then climbs through the Bois de la Côte to join the Pré Sergent, then the hamlet of Les Alliés.

Le Théverot
950m

After the last Théverot farms, the GR5 continues on the tarmac road, which soon gives way to a forest track climbing on the left bank of the mountain torrent. By the "chez Blaiset" Farm, situated in Swiss territory, you bear right skirting a walled enclosure, then find a path climbing the hillside up to two ancient farm-houses situated astride the border at 1,200m.

Continue in the same south westerly direction

Montbenoît

Everything combines to make the Abbey of Montbenoît, formerly the county-town of the Val de Saugeais, the hub of the Haut-Doubs: its isolation at a height of almost 800 metres, amid "tué" farms; its peerless religious architecture in this mountain region; the antiquity of its foundation by the Sire de Joux in 1150.

The church dates from the 12th, 14th and 16th centuries. It is to Ferry Carondelet, abbé commandataire from 1522 to 1527 and adviser to Charles V, that the flamboyant decoration of the choir and the famous stalls, ornamented with remarkable finesse on satirical themes, are due. The adjoining cloister, which one would have thought Romanesque, was built in 1439 in a much earlier style. As soon as you go in, you are impressed by the harmony of its proportions, by the intimacy it conveys, by the simplicity of its double-colonetted capitals, decorated with motifs taken from the flora and fauna of the mountains. In one corner of the cloister, some steps lead to a vaulted room in which old Comtois furniture gleams in the half-light. From the grand style to rustic simplicity, Montbenoît thus encompasses every aspect of the region's soul.

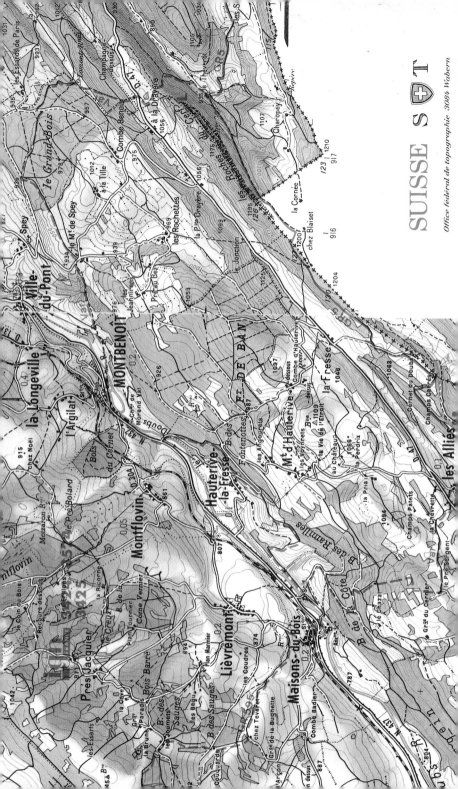

SUISSE S T

Office fédéral de topographie 3084 Wabern

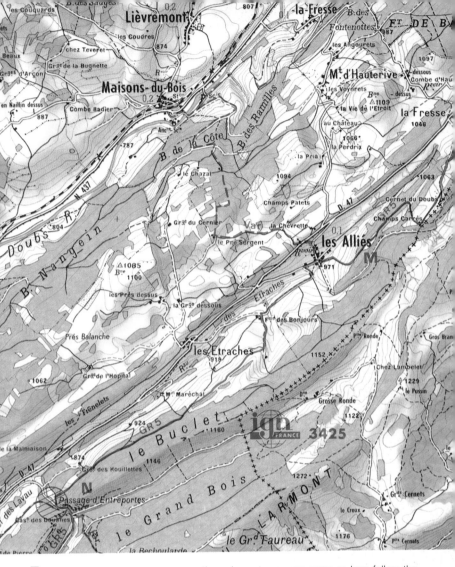

through pastures; you more or less follow the frontier on the French side, as far as the "Cernet du Doubs " farms at 1,150m. Next, continue along the edge of the ravine and the border markers, then bear right or north west to skirt round a fir plantation, entry to which is prohibited; follow the frontier wall, then the edge of the tree nursery; the path becomes stony, and bends left to the bottom of the ravine. Take the forest path going downstream and follow it as far as Les Alliés.

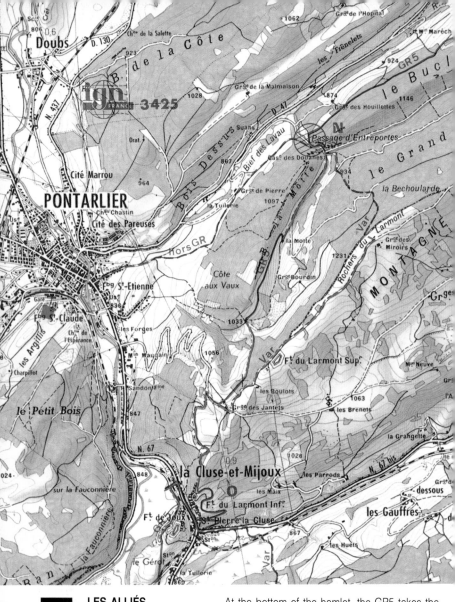

LES ALLIÉS
🏠 🍴
950m

At the bottom of the hamlet, the GR5 takes the D47 in the direction of Pontarlier; 250 metres further on, turn left, cross the Étraches stream and turn right on to the path leading to the Bonjours Farm. Before the buildings bear right or south west on a path into a pasture. Follow the waymarking carefully as there is no visible path. Continue through pastures on the edge of a spinney, then go into the Charbonnière woods. Carefully close the gates after you on this stretch. Leaving the woods, bear left to descend to the tarmac road to the Entreportes Crossing at 880m.

6Km
1:45

Detour *1:00*
PONTARLIER
🏠 🏕 ✕ 🚉 🚃 🚌
840m

Detour see left. Cross the road and, almost opposite, take a track climbing into the woods; shortly after, when you leave them, the track bears left and descends to a treeless area. After the "Grange de Pierre", the track turns right descending as far as Pontarlier.

The GR5 takes the road left to climb to the Entreportes Crossing.

Entreportes crossing
890m

The walker can take either of two routes to reach La Cluse-et-Mijoux: an Alternative route via Les Rochers du Larmont, with a section over a tarmac road or the GR5, which remains on the mountainside.

Alternative route by Rochers du Larmont. At the Entreportes Crossing, the alternative route takes the gravelled road climbing east, behind the old Customs shed; at a hairpin bend, take a short steep path. The path skirts the edge of a small ravine worn away by an intermittent mountain stream; you cut across a road and the gradient becomes less pronounced. You reach Les Rochers du Larmont which, at 1,230m, tower some 300m above the Entreportes defile. From the crest, go to the right on the tourist road. You pass in front of a hôtel at Fort Larmont Supérieur, and reach Grange des Jantets.

6Km
1:45

A ski resort in winter.

ENTREPORTES CROSSING

The GR5, at the Entreportes Crossing, takes the right-hand track. Open a gate, taking care to close it securely; the track climbs up into a combe; you pass it and go on above the La Motte Farm, still flanking the hillside. You come out into a large pasture, which you cross as you make for the dirt road which you spot in the distance, and which climbs up to Grange des Jantets.

4Km
1:00

GRANGE DES JANTETS
🏠 ✕
1,096m
Unattended gîte.
Junction with the GR5.

2Km
0:30

Pass in front of the buildings and, for a short distance, follow the tarmac road heading down towards Pontarlier, then take a track on the left crossing some pastures, follow the cliff dominating the Doubs Valley, and you arrive at Fort Larmont Inférieur.

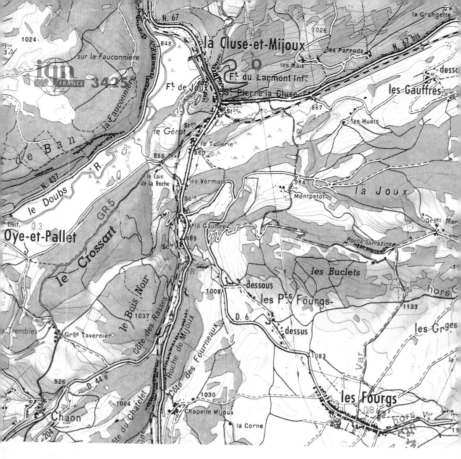

Fort Larmont Inférieur
Situated above the town of La Cluse-et-Mijoux.

10Km
2:30

The GR5 descends into the town, but walkers can choose between two possible routes, to Les Hôpitaux-Neufs: an alternative route by La Roche Sarrazine, and Les Fourgs (the highest village in the region), or by the GR5 by Montperreux and Malbuisson.

Alternative route by La Roche Sarrazine. At Fort Larmont Inférieur, on the right of the ramparts, bear left and take the track winding downhill to the church. When you reach the N67 bis Neuchâtel road, follow it left for 500 metres; at the last house, turn right onto a dirt road passing beneath the railway; 200 metres further on, it gives way to a path skirting a pasture where you should stay at the edge of the fence; at the far end, climb some stairs and continue straight ahead to enter the forest and reach the hamlet of Montpetot. Take the tarmac road leading to the houses, pass in front of the chapel and a fountain, and bear

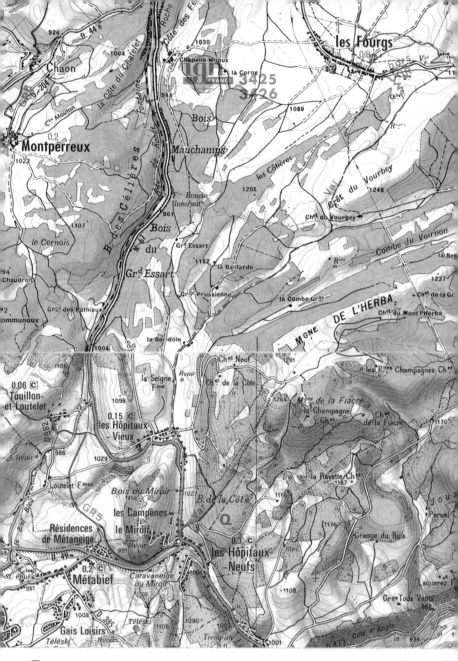

left. The GR skirts a farm, then enters a pasture; follow the fencing on the left and, still climbing, you reach the forest, where the track can be made out clearly again; follow it as far as the entrance to a large pasture; here, bear left and climb the hillside to come on to an

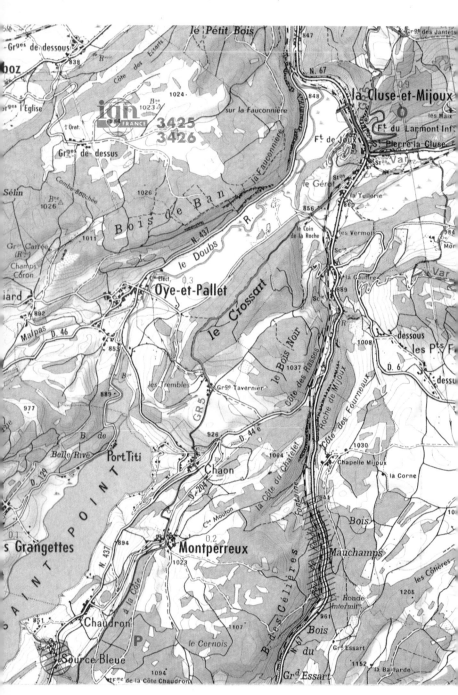

200 metres away, do not miss the Roche Sarrazine view point.

LES FOURGS
🏠 ⌂ 🍴 ⛲

1,100m
Highest village in Doubs Départment.

10Km
2:30

Fort Larmont Inférieur

2Km
0:30

LA CLUSE-ET-MIJOUX
🏠 🍴

860m
Taking the N67 left, you find some café-restaurants. Hôtel on the N67 by the hamlet of La Tuilerie (in the south part of the town).
5 kilometres from Pontarlier, situated on major route between Besançon and Switzerland; dominated by Fort de Joux, at 940m on steep rock overhanging famous Pontarlier transverse valley by 200 metres.

8Km
2:00

MONTPERREUX
🏠 ⌂

990m

à Chaudron

excellent forest track which you follow for 2 kilometres to the Grange sur la Roche Farm. The GR takes the commune road (closed to traffic) as far as the village.

In Les Fourgs, turn left and climb the main RD6 road again as far as the cross, where you leave the road to walk along a winding path flanking the hillside, as far as the Chapelle du Tourillet which comes into view. Continue behind the chapel to reach a dirt road leading to the Vourbey ridge (it is not advisable to climb to the summit, on which a high tension pylon has been set up). Follow the electricity line as far as a lodge, the "Vuillaumes" (1197m), and descend by the forest track which, below and turning left, leads to Les Hôpitaux-Neufs.

At the Fort du Larmont Inférieur, the GR rounds the fort to the south as far as the view point situated at the south west corner. You overlook La Cluse-et-Mijoux. Descend by a winding track, then by stairways as far as the N67 and La Cluse-et-Mijoux.

When you arrive at the N67 turn right and skirt the N67 for 300 metres along the pavement. At the first houses, bear left, go over the level crossing and turn left again. After 300 metres, take the stairway leaving the village and the footpath leading to the château. Descend again by the one-way road; 200 metres further on, turn right downhill along a path, go over a bridge, leave the road behind and continue opposite. You climb over the crest of Mount Crossard through some felling areas. Over the wooded crest, the GR follows a good track opening out on to a road which you follow left as far as some buildings named the Grange de Tavernier at 929m; at the crossroads turn right or south and descend as far as Chaon. Take the road climbing to the D44 which you cross to turn right on to a road which 800 metres further on joins the D44, which you take right to enter the village of Montperreux.

The GR leaves the village heading for Chaudron. 100 metres away, it heads left or west on a horizontal lane which ends at a road

above Chaudron. Follow this upwards for about 100 metres, then descend down a widened slope along the edge of meadows, skirting a barbed wire fence. The path continues along the edge of a wood, climbs a little way and passes near La Source Bleue.

After La Source Bleue, the GR5 cuts across the first tarmac road, then by a short steep incline you come into a second road which you take right (south west) downhill; finally, you turn left into a lane arriving at Malbuisson.

The GR does not enter the village but turns left after a tennis court; you pass in front of a chalet, "La Biche" and 50 metres further on, turn left and climb a forest track over the hill dominating Malbuisson. You skirt some meadows, cross a tarmac road and continue between two conifer woods. After crossing a cleared area, you again enter a wood which you cross paying close attention to waymarkings. You come out on to a plateau divided into pastures, which you cross closing gates behind you until you reach the hamlet of Touillon-et-Loutelet. At the entrance to the hamlet, turn right then left at the transformer; you cut across the D45 and reach the ballast of an old railway which you follow right or south. You cross a small combe and 500 metres further on, you pass a track on the right going to Métabief.

Continue along the ballast of the old railway to reach Les Hôpitaux-Neufs.

Warning For the next 25 kilometres, until Mouthe, the GR does not pass through any villages. Pay close attention to the waymarking.

The GR5 leaves Les Hôpitaux-Neufs passing in front of the gendarmerie, to join a track which goes sideways up the slope which you can see from the village. You cross some meadows and a fir plantation; you cut across the forest road climbing from Métabief to Le Morond, then you climb flanking the hillside along a

---

4Km
1:00

MALBUISSON
890m
Pleasant village situated on edge of Lake Saint-Point; large leisure centre: tennis, sailing, water skiing, fishing, horse riding, "petanque", promenades; much frequented during the summer season.

8Km
2:30

Detour 0:15mins
MÉTABIEF
950m

LES HOPITAUX-NEUFS
990m
Summer holiday resort; winter sports centre.

5Km
1:30

path in the fir forest to meet the forest road, which you again cut across. You continue flanking the hillside to meet some pastures. You then follow the edge of the cliff parallel with the ski lifts and cable cars, and climb to Le Morond.

LE MOROND
⌂
1,420m

The GR descends again into a combe.

Descend south and cross a combe, then through a vast mountain pasture towards the Mont d'Or overhang. Do not get too close to the edge of the dangerous cliffs (especially in foggy weather). The GR5 continues south along the skyline, still keeping back from the cliff, until you reach a turnstile to get through a wall marking a property boundary. Here turn sharp right or west and skirt the wall going downhill.

View over Dent de Vaulion and Mont Tendre.

The GR joins a forest track (pay close attention to waymarking), then cuts across a power line which you follow west, passing in turn in front of the chalets of La Coquille, La Blonay and Le Chalet de Boissaude.

CHALET LA BOISSAUDE
✗

As far as Mouthe, GR passes large alpine farm-houses where, in event of bad weather, shelter can be easily found and, very often, accommodation.

12Km
3:30

Still heading west, the GR5 reaches the Besaine Farm. When the power line turns right or north continue straight ahead following the markings on trees; you descend through a meadow-wood as far as a road which you take right. Pass in front of the Granges Raguin and 100 metres further on, turn left or south on to a gravelled track on the edge of a fir plantation. You arrive at the Corneau chalet. To the right of the chalet, take a track over the bare limestone. Stay in the wood as far as a narrow clearing. The path passes by a filled up well, crosses the clearing and a dry-stone wall, turns right and up into the wood again. Follow a track, then take a forest path left leading to the clearing at the Vannot barn, nicknamed the "Hôtel des Sauvages". The GR passes below the chalet, heads towards a large solitary tree, and crosses the pasture in the direction of a gap provided in a dry-stone wall. Continue bearing west through a meadow-wood. You enter the forest again passing a track on the right which descends into a fir plantation. The path, proceeding on an incline, reaches the La Grange-Bousson clearing.

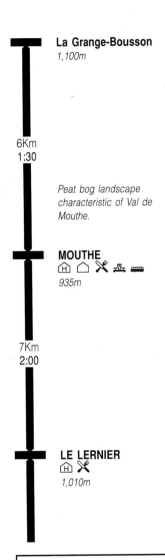

La Grange-Bousson
1,100m

6Km
1:30

*Peat bog landscape
characteristic of Val de
Mouthe.*

MOUTHE
935m

7Km
2:00

LE LERNIER
1,010m

The GR continues westward, skirts some heaps of stones, arrives at the forest again and comes in view of the Sapeau Léger. From here, along a good path, you reach a tarmac road which you follow right or west. You pass a road climbing left and reach a hairpin bend. Right into the bend take the first track, which descends into a fir plantation, then to the edge of it. You come out again on to a hairpin bend in a road; take this road right.

After a few hundred metres, the GR turns left or south west to reach the base of the source of the Doubs. From the car park, it takes the road for Mouthe.

The GR5 leaves Mouthe by the D437 in the direction of Petite-Chaux; about 1 kilometre past the last houses, turn left on to the first by-road you meet; 300 metres further on, turn right or south west to climb up to the road coming from Petite-Chaux. Continue for 2 kilometres along this small road in the same direction; and after a hairpin bend, when it heads south east, continue straight ahead, first through undergrowth, then along the edge and finally along the ridge as far as the Champans Farm. The GR joins the Chaux-Neuve road on a bend and descends to arrive at the hamlet of Le Lernier.

At the large bend in the road at the Le Lernier houses, the GR turns west south west on to a track climbing to the base of a combe. When you reach the topographic col, a marked beech-tree, cut across to the right slope taking the shortest route, go into a fir plantation and turn on to a good ridge track. After leaving the

Little Siberia
Mouthe is mentioned on the radio stations, every winter morning, as the coldest place in France. This large market town, nicknamed the "Siberia of the Haut-Doubs" shares this unenviable distinction with l'Abbaye-en-Grandvaux and the hamlet of Brévine, in the Swiss Jura. In these places the thermometer regularly drops to -30°. In 1888, on the night of 31 January/1st February, it even registered -48°. Despite these polar temperatures, the climate of the Haut-Pays is considered to be one of the healthiest in Europe. Demographic statistics bear out that the people there tend to live to be very old.

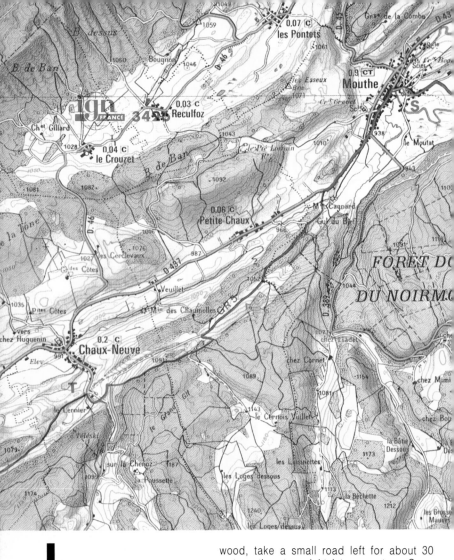

13Km
4:00

Chez l'Officier

wood, take a small road left for about 30 metres, then turn right into a pasture. Cross this, diagonally, bearing towards the left slope of the combe where there are some ruins. An old track at the edge of the wood, skirts the clearing and comes out on a crossroad by several farms. Take the road left; it winds upwards through the Bannal Wood and terminates after 1 hour's walk in the crescent-shaped clearing named Chez l'Officier.

In the clearing, the GR bears right, in a south westerly direction over a wide grassy track, alternatively crossing woods and clearings, skirts a dell then ends in the lozenge-shaped

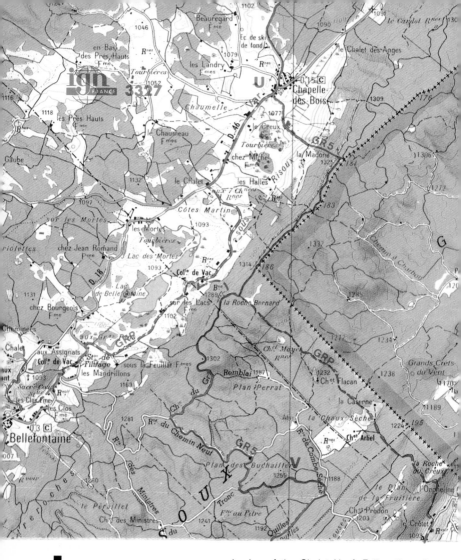

clearing of the Chalet Neuf. Follow the edge, then leave the main track and descend right or south on a forest footpath which arrives at a ledge notable for the absence of any trees on it. From here, make for a mound in the middle of which a well has been built. Following the waymarking, you reach a forestry development track which opens out on to an enormous roundabout at which a road terminates. The GR takes this road as far as a crossroads, turns left, passes near the chalets of Nondances and reaches Chapelle-des-Bois.

CHAPELLE-DES-BOIS

🏠 ⌂ ✕ ⚏

1,080m

Detour

A detour leads you to the "Tour of the Lakes" GR559, passing by Combe David, Maison Neuve, Les Serettes.

FONCINE-LE-BAS

🏠 ✕ ⚏

4Km
1:30

The Malvaux Gorges, Les Planches-en-Montagne, the Langouette Waterfall, La Loye.

CHAUX-DE-CROTENAY

🏠 ✕ ⚏

Les Grassets, Morillon, the Chevrières Viaduct, Bans wood and the Petit-Maclu lake on the GR559.

CHAPELLE-DES-BOIS

4Km
1:45

La Roche Bernard

1,289m
Junction with the GR5.
View over Lake Bellefontaine.

4Km
1:00

From here there are two routes to reach La Roche Bernard: the alternative route, over the small road, and the GR5 by the frontier ridge.

Alternative route by the road. At the last houses in Chapelle-des-Bois, follow the D46 for 2 kilometres. A few hundred metres past the Michel Distillerie, turn left on to a small road. 2 kilometres further on, by two farms, the GR turns on to the very steep hillside to reach the La Roche Bernard view point.

The GR5 leaves Chapelle-des-Bois by the D46 heading for Morez. At the last houses, it turns left or south east on to a gravelled road which it follows for 1 kilometre. Bear left or north east, cross a fence and through pasture-woods you reach the edge of the forest. Here, turn right or east on a path winding up beneath some woods to reach the ridge. Continue on the latter in a south westerly direction; you pass near the Risoux cross or the Roche Champion view point at 1,326m. The path continues between the cliff edge and the line of the frontier, and reaches a larger road which you take to the right for some metres, which you then leave to proceed to the La Roche Bernard view point.

A little further on, the GR leaves the Doubs département to enter the Jura. It passes through the vast Forest of Risoux covering more than 3,000 hectares. The GR moves away from La Roche Bernard, heading south in the Morez forest; it then goes into Morbier Forest and follows an unloading track, the boundary of parcels 2 and 3, which ends at the gravelled forest road of Grand-Remblai. Take the road right or south west. 100 metres away, on the right, is Grand-Remblai forest hut, open to walkers. Follow the road for 1 kilometre

to reach the Chemin Neuf road crossroads. The GR turns left or south west. About 1.3 kilometres further on, it arrives by a tarmac road at Plan des Buchaillers.

Plan des Buchaillers

⌂

1,216m

Detour

taking the road left or north east for 1 kilometre, you come across a forest hut at the side of the road.

The GR turns right or south and takes the Croix du Tronc road.

Then, at the Plan des Buchaillers, the GR turns right and takes the La Croix du Tronc road; 600 metres further on, it leaves it for the Clovis track which it takes left.

2Km
0:30

Detour

Continuing along the La Croix du Tronc road, south west, you find 1,500 metres further on, two "Chalets des Ministres" forest huts (8 persons each) open all the year round.

1,400 metres further on, you come out on to the Route de la Combe Sèche or Chaux Sèche track: the GR then turns right or south and 100 metres further on, it reaches the Route de la Combette-aux-Quilles.

ROUTE DE LA COMBETTE-AUX-QUILLES

3.5Km
0:45

⌂

The GR takes this road left or south west to the Carrefour de la Biche.

Carrefour de la Biche

1,228m

Junction with the Étroit road.

Detour *1:00*

BOIS D'AMONT

1,075m

Follow the Étroit road downhill.

Continue on the Combette road; 500 metres after the La Biche crossroads, you reach the Rose chalet (forest hut). 1 kilometre further on, when the road bends left, continue straight ahead along a forest track called the "Petites-Croix track". You pass a cross. Pay close attention to the waymarking, since three times the GR leaves the visible track to take short-cuts.

You come out on the Crêt-des-Sauges forest road, which you take left. A little further on, turn right on to a track terminating at the Long Chemin, gravelled forest road.

9Km
2:15

The GR crosses the road and takes a track which bears left or south, almost opposite. You then come to the foot of the Gros Crétet.

Gros Crétet

Relay transmitter on summit.

Under the Gros Crétet relay transmitter, the GR5 drops steeply down a short path to meet the forest road; when it turns left or east go

LES ROUSSES

1,080m

🏠 ⌂ ✕ 🚊 🚌

Summer tourist centre and winter sports resort; south west of town, is Fort des Rousses, begun in 1834 for the defence of crossing between Faucille and Saint-Cergue cols, and Orbe, Bienne and Valserine valleys.

3Km
0:45

Le Bief de la Chaille Youth Hostel

1,041m

Crossing point of GR9 which comes from Mijoux (see GR9 Topoguide from Saint-Amour to Mijoux); GR9 and GR5 share same route as far as D29 road.

2Km
0:30

D29 Road

GR5 and GR9 part; GR9 takes road south.

Detour *15 mins*

By the GR9, in 15 minutes, you reach the Loge de Beauregard gîte d'étape.

2Km
0:30

LA CURE

⌂ ✕ 🚌 🚋

1,150m

Hamlet situated on the Swiss frontier.

right to come upon a track which you follow right or south west for about 350 metres. The GR curves left or south and through pastures and woods reaches Les Rousses.

The GRP joins the GR5 in front of the creamery where you follow the red and white markings. After crossing the town, at the end of the housing estate, the GRP crosses a property, joins a commune service road and follows this to the hamlet of Sagy-le-Haut. By the last house, take the track right which goes down through a clearing then into the forest. 200 metres further on, descend right, down a slight gradient. When the track takes a sharp bend right, continue straight on, then gradually climb up again to the Le Bief de la Chaille road. Follow the latter right for 400 metres.

Continue along the road, then by a group of houses, turn right or south on to a small road going down to the Guyot windmill and cross the Le Bief de la Chaille stream. The path then winds between some fenced meadows and climbs towards Les Cressonières to terminate at the D29 Road.

The GR5 takes the D29 road left or east heading for the hamlet of La Cure.

The route of the GR5 continues on Swiss territory and is signposted. The waymarkings are yellow painted lozenges or bars.

Then, after the La Cure Customs post, head for the station and take a road right leading to the cantonal road where the traffic often is quite heavy; follow it for 500 metres, then turn left on to the old road. You reach the railway which you skirt for a hundred or so metres. You come to the road again and cross it to take a forest track which enters the La Pile wood; 1 kilometre further on, turn right (you pass the

road on the left going to the Col de la Givrine). You come out at the La Pile-Dessus chalet. Turn sharp left, here, and head across the pasture towards a small wood to the south east.

9Km
2:15

Formerly, frontier followed bottom of the Dappes combe, but there was a swap of territories to enable France to build a road from La Cure to La Faucille, Switzerland receiving equivalent area further north; opposite, north side of the Dôle with Geneva-Cointrin intercontinental airport ASR and the short-wave antenna.

At the edge of the wood, you find a track which you follow for 500 metres where you come upon a crossroads: leave the road which heads north east to join the major road, turning right or south to reach a small road which you follow north east. Further on, pass the Trélasse chalet which you glimpse on the left; continue as far as the hamlet of Couvaloup-de-Saint-Cergue. The GR5 then descends in the same direction, as far as the hamlet of Saint-Cergue.

In this hamlet, bearing south, you find Balcon du Léman GR; by following this GR southwards, you can climb to summit of Barillette, with view-point over Alps and Lake Geneva; television antenna serving the whole of French-speaking region.

Then, in the hamlet of Saint-Cergue, the GR5 passes the Barillette chairlift road on the right or south, and continues heading east. Its route is the same as the E4 European footpath and the Balcon du Léman GR, as far as Saint-Cergue. Then, by La Chanelette, you arrive at Les Chésaux: to avoid falling back on to the major road and the Guinfard road, take the old road as far as the centre of the village of Saint-Cergue.

SAINT-CERGUE
⌂ ✕ 🚉 🚌

1,040m
Junction of the GR5, which is also European path No. 2, and the Pyrenees-Austria European path No. 4.

The GR5 leaves Saint-Cergue by the cantonal road in the direction of Nyon; 600 metres further on, it turns left along a descending track.

11Km
2:40

This track is a part of the Roman road linking Nyon to ...Paris. Remains of this track can be seen over about 2 kilometres, since the GR5 takes this road. The descent is a pleasant one, in the summer shade, as you follow the old Roman road, paved with its large cobbles; beautiful vistas over Lake Geneva and the Alps.

The track cuts across the road, which winds in great loops, on six occasions.

The forest is a mix of firs and beeches. At the foot of the forest, you come to a road which you follow for 2.5 kilometres as far as Trélex. This is the old, little frequented Nyon to Saint-Cergue road, a new road having been built further west.

The Haut Jura in Winter

In winter Haut Jura is traditionally the land of cold and snow. From St-Claude to Maîche, from Delémont to Saint-Cergue, the "montagnons" are only happy when a winter really is a winter. For centuries, Jura villages scattered along the frontier have remained completely isolated for at least five months of the year. All the roads are blocked by enormous snowdrifts, in some places reaching heights of five or six metres. In the Haut-Pays, life was then organised at a slower pace and, thanks to the self-contained independence of families, people and animals subsisted on the provisions amassed during the fine weather. For road communications between farms, you first used a rudimentary clearing procedure hitching cattle to tree trunks which you simply dragged over the snow. Then, you started to build some type of stem-posts with beams and planks, heavy triangles which twenty horses would heave along with great difficulty, sinking in up to their breast, over the roads of the Joux Valley or the Mouthe region. Often, overnight, another storm would obliterate all their efforts, and they would have to start all over again. With these snow ploughs only operating on the main roads, farming folk would have to shift for themselves to link up their own dwelling to the road that had been cleared. They would shovel away for days on end to keep open these narrow alleys, which the wind would take malicious pleasure in covering over again.

ANDRÉ BESSON "MON PAYS COMTOIS" PUBLISHED BY FRANCE-EMPIRE

Leaving the forest, broad panorama comes in view, as far as Nyon: countryside, lake and Alps of Savoy.

Cross Trélex, go east of the station and take a pleasant little track. Below the cemetery, turn left and cross a wide, flat, bare expanse of ground. After passing under the motorway, you cross the Calèves estate to meet the road at the entrance to Nyon.

NYON

375m
Town in canton of Vaud at edge of Lake Geneva. Old 12th and 15th century churches, 12th century choir. Roman antiquities.

THE REGION OF MONTBÉLIARD

The Montbéliard Region GR takes the shape of a 140 kilometre loop, with its departure point in Vandoncourt. Why Vandoncourt?...You really have to start from somewhere and it seemed to us that this small town, the nearest to the Montbéliard area, represented the ideal spot given:

- its location near the Lomont,
- its quintessentially rural character,
- its dynamism, its gîtes d'étape and
- its tradition of hospitality.

Situation and Relief

The Montbéliard Region is situated between the last upthrusts of the Vosges and the northern tip of the Jura. It forms an open crossing both into the rich plain of Alsace and into Burgundy; eastwards, it touches Switzerland and in the south, on the Lomont, it joins the Jura: it is a limestone ridge which reaches 868m at Montcheroux and 930m at Montancy. From here, two wide plateaux, separated by the corridor hewn by the Doubs, descend in an easy slope towards the plain in which the busy area of Montbéliard is situated. The path extends somewhat beyond the "region" and reaches the first foothills of the Haut-Doubs at Belleherbe.

The Economy of the Region

The economy is basically centred on the Peugeot factories, an industrial complex taking in 260 hectares between Sochaux and Montbéliard and employing some 36,000 workers. By way of spin-offs, a large network of companies located in the industrial areas of the town has been created and provides a livelihood for thousands. The Montbéliard Region thus constitutes a pool of labour, a large proportion of which is employed at Peugeot.

The History of the Region

The attraction of this charming Region goes back to much more distant times. Well before our era, the ancient tribe of the Sequani followed the religion of the druids, as the stones and tumuli left in Hérimoncourt testify. The Roman colonisers had fully appreciated the value of this site, since they built there the great Gallo-Roman city of Epomanduodurum (Mandeure), on the edge of the Doubs and the Blamont Plateau. The arrival of Christianity and the great invasions also frequently left behind traces of legend, like the Sarrazin Bridge of Vandoncourt. And the industrialization of the 19th century and the two World Wars, cruelly affecting the Region, must not lead us to forget the powerful fortresses erected in the Middle Ages on the two sides of the Lomont, as at Blamont, Belvoir and Montjoie-le-Château.

The Forest

This is chiefly composed of three species: spruce, beech and oak. The last two generally grow below an altitude of 800m while spruce prevails above it. The greenery of the oaks and beeches, the pastures and orchards, combine with the warm colours of the cultivated soils, the area of which increases, the further down towards the plain you go. There are abundant orchards surrounding the houses, the fruit trees yielding some fine produce: apple trees, plum and mirabelle plum trees grow virtually everywhere; pear, peach and walnut trees are less common.

The Rivers

The largest is the Doubs, which twice crosses the Department, but flows only over 40 or so kilometres in the Montbéliard Region. It enters Switzerland as far as Sainte-Ursanne, and then, heading sharply east to west, it re-enters the region through the picturesque Val de Glère-Vaufrey and cuts across the Lomont range, forming a clearly drawn transverse valley, in which Saint-Hippolyte nestles. Further on, descending northwards, it waters Pont-de-Roide and reaches 3 kilometres south of Montbéliard, before heading south east for Besançon. The Dessoubre joins the Doubs at Saint-Hippolyte. A river of the first order, it is an angler's paradise, as is the Doubs in the Val de Glère.

Gastronomy

A region of enchantment for tourists, Franche-Comté also offers gourmets the most delectable, local dishes. Mention must first be made of its two best known cheeses: the Comté and Cancoillote or "colle" as the people of the region call it. The other mainstay of the cuisine is smoked meat. This tradition goes back to previous generations who were obliged to find a means of preserving meats through our long winters. Thus, in Franche-Comté, you smoke ham, lard,... and, of course, the famous Montbéliard sausage.

Advice and information on Walking the Montbéliard Region.

The GR of the Montbéliard Region is waymarked with two painted bars, yellow and red; in the section shared with the GR5, these two lines are red and white.

The Regional GR is set beside the GR5 for 20 kilometres of its route between Saint-Hippolyte and Vandoncourt. The route takes the "Customs path" astride the Franco-Swiss frontier. So you are advised to carry your identity card and, walkers accompanied by a dog should have the dog's anti-rabies vaccination certificate, less than three months old.

During the hunting season, it is advisable to stay close to the path and not go into the wood.

It should be pointed out that the walker will, throughout the whole of his journey and in virtually all of the villages crossed, find "fruitières" or creameries, in which the delicious "Comté" cheese is produced, on which the fame of our province is built.

WALK 3

VANDONCOURT
△ ✕ ⚓

400m
Sarrazin Bridge: according to
legend, in the 8th century,
the village, galvanized by
Vaddo, rose up against the
Saracen invader.

4Km
1:00

In front of the cemetery, the
Regional GR and GR5
diverge: the GR5 continues
right or north towards Dasle.

From the centre of the village, follow the red and white GR5 waymarking, climb up the Rue de Dasle, then turn left at the last house.

The Regional GR (red and yellow waymarking) continues straight ahead west over a well-marked track through fields. A little before Seloncourt, it enters a pasture. There are no waymarkings for 500 metres. Close the gates securely. You enter the village of Seloncourt.

SELONCOURT
✕ ⚓ ===

350m
Protestant church.

5Km
1:30

At the Place du Marché, turn left into the main street for 50 metres, then into the Rue de la Lanne, and the Rue Neuve which takes you to the Chapel; climb the Rue du Château d'Eau left. A short way after the cemetery, the Regional GR turns right into the wood; it then reaches the Rue des Combes, enters the Esssart Bourguignon wood soon afterwards, and leads to the place called *Les Cinq Sapins*. After leaving the wood by a track south you reach Thulay.

THULAY
✕

500m

In the town, turn right after the first bend; 1 kilometre on, the road makes a bend right; go straight ahead along the edge for 300m, then turn left into the wood. The Regional GR thus joins the D35 by the Haut des Bois Farm, cuts across it and opposite goes into the spruce plantation where there are 500 metres without waymarkings. The path goes into a beech grove. After going downhill, you reach the fields above Beaulieu. Climb the first track left into a forest felling or clear felling area.

Beautiful view in the direction
of Montbéliard and its
13Km *environs.*
4:00 *View over Montbéliard.*

On the shoulder, turn right to join the "Combe de la Bourdelotte" road. Go down as far as the houses and follow the combe in the direction of the forest. At the next crossing, climb right by the steepest path, then a track leading to Côte Jeanney.

View over Montbéliard.

You cut across two roads and arrive at a clearing called Rond Chatelet.

Relaxation and picnic area.

Then follow a track right or north east passing under a high tension line, turn north west, then north and reach the Mandeure view point.

Relaxation and picnic area.

By a picturesque path you skirt the cliff, then go down as far as the Roman theatre of Mandeure. Take the road right leading to the entrance to Mandeure.

MANDEURE

340m
Mandeure (or Epomanduodurum) was the second Roman city of the Region after Vesontio (Besançon); it was rich and prosperous with monumental marble-lined public baths, and its great ancient theatre, now partially restored. The theatre could hold up to 12,000 people; it was the second largest theatre of the Gauls, larger than the theatre of Orange.

3Km
1:00

The GR turns left on to the N437, crosses the Doubs and turns right immediately after the bridge; it then takes the dirt road heading for the forest. Turn right on to the second road and 20 metres after the level crossing, take the gravelled road left. Along this, skirt the railway as far as the tunnel, then continue straight ahead. You reach the Equestrian Centre of Les Aigreviers.

LES AIGREVIERS

View over Mandeure and Doubs Valley.

6Km
1:45

The GR follows the tarmac road, cuts across the N438 and opposite goes into the Mathay wood. Continue along the road left as far as the Combe des Cerfs (not mentioned on the map); climb up right again into the pasture, then descend again on the other side of the meadow skirting the southern edge. Do not leave it again until the end of the pasture. The GR then takes the CD475 on the left; it leaves it 700 metres further on, to turn right through undergrowth, on to a gravelled track climbing to Écot.

ÉCOT

530m
The village suffered grievously during the last war: a monument dedicated to the "maquis" of Écot

2.5Km
0:40

Turn left near the church on to the D123; 100 metres further on, turn right on to a track which, from the heights descends to Villars-sous-Écot.

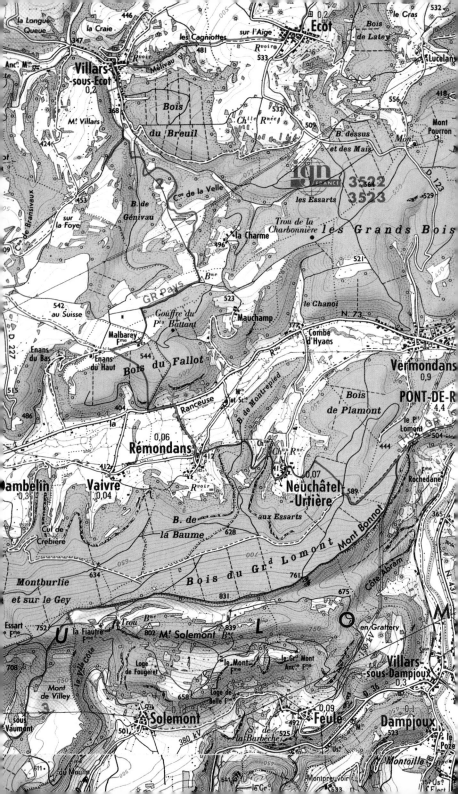

commemorates the difficult
times it knew during this
period. Also noteworthy is a
modern church in an "avant-
garde" style.
Pretty view over neighbouring
hills.

Villars-sous-Écot
365m
*Site of a tragic episode in
the Resistance; on 19
September 1944, all the men
of the parish were shot by
the Germans.*

6Km
1:30

At the foot of the village, the path takes the
CD265 left for 300 metres, then heads for the
sports ground below; it skirts the stadium,
crosses the stream and takes the track left
along it. At the next crossroads, continue on
the edge of the wood, as far as the felling area
on the left; climb the hill, to reach a gravelled
road higher up; cross the cattle grid and do
not leave this track again. The path then
reaches a peak of the Écot Plateau where
there is an IGN marker. The GR then bears
south west as far as the Malbarey Farm; about
500 metres past the farm, it leaves the road
and turns left into the Le Fallot Wood. Descend
to the N73 in the Ranceuse Valley. Turn left on
to the road, then right at the next crossing, to
arrive at Rémondans.

Rémondans
410m

The Regional GR climbs the first street in the
village, to the left, then up the track it leads on
to. You thus reach the ruins of the feudal
château of Neuchâtel-Urtière.

2.5Km
0:40

*At foot of château, small
chapel with unusual 16th
century altar-piece (key from
mayor).*

Continue on the same track to the bottom of
the Neuchâtel-Urtière blind valley.

Neuchâtel-Urtière
415m
*Formerly, a typical small
market town dominated by a
château belonging to the
Montfaucon, then the
Neuchais families; it rose
above a rocky ridge
overhanging by some ten or
so metres the boulevard,
around which stood the
houses of the town. In the
12th century, it was a real
stronghold, although today*

3Km
0:45

The Regional GR turns right in the middle of
the village, then left, at the edge of the wood,
to climb a wide, very steep track; it comes out
at a vast clearing, crosses it and joins the
Pont-de-Roide to Dambelin forest track: follow it
north east for 1 kilometre. Here, the GR leaves
the forest track to turn right at a sharp angle
on to a track climbing to the ridge.

only a few ruins remain, largely overrun by nature's pervasive inroads (cf Franche-Comté Region of 24.7.81).

Petit-Lomont Locality
444m
Detour *40 mins*
PONT-DE-ROIDE
⌂ ✖ ⚖

350m
Continue along the road in a north easterly direction. Short walking tour of 10 kilometres, "Les Roches", leaves from Community Centre.

10Km
2:45

Beautiful views of the Valley of Doubs at Pont-de-Roide and over Barbèche Valley.

Valonne
530m

Then, exiting the wood, the GR leaves the forest track to turn right or south west, at an acute angle, on to a ridge path, which it follows to Valonne.

The route follows the Lomont Ridge as far as the west end of the pastures of the La Fiautre farm, skirts round them by the forest and joins the access road to La Fiautre: turn right on to it and follow it downhill as far as Valonne.

The Regional GR takes the D36 towards Vyt-les-Belvoir, then the track right after the "Valonne" sign; it then reaches the forest and pastures on the ridge. Follow the gravelled track as far as the Lomont Farm, then the access road to it for 250 metres; fork right on the edge of the forest with the PTT antenna on left, and turn into the field in the direction of the television antenna or due west.

Caution not much in the way of waymarking from the edge of the wood to the television antenna.

At 850m, this is the high point of the Montbéliard Region GR and the French part of Lomont Range providing a splendid view: to the north, over the Vosges, the Montbéliard Region, the Belfort Gap and the Plain of Alsace; to the South, over the Jura mountains, the Bernese Alps and, in fine

12Km
3:00

The GR leaves the heights by the access road to the antenna, which joins the D36; take this road right and, 500 metres further on, take the first dirt road left called the "Cassepouille".

weather, over the Mont Blanc Massif.

Remains of Roman road built 2,000 years ago.

You descend to Rahon.

RAHON
⌂
550m

2Km
0:40

On the D31, at the entrance to Rahon, turn left, then 30 metres on, right towards Belvoir; continue on the road for 700 metres and climb left towards Chapelle Sainte-Anne. At the foot of it, take the track right flanking the hillside which leads to the upper end of Belvoir.

Belvoir
✕
600m

2.5Km
0:30

At the port-cullis of the château, descend left to the foot of the village; by the restaurant, go left again and after passing the last house in the village, turn right; you are on an old Roman road which leads to Sancey-le-Long.

SANCEY-LE-LONG
⚓ ✕
500m
A leap in time brings us back from the Middle Ages to the beginning of our own century, when the curious Romanesque basilica was built, plumb in the middle of the village. It was designed by the architect, Abram, in honour of St Jeanne-Antide Thouret, founder of the order of the Sisters of Charity.

5.5Km
1:30

The GR cuts across the N464, crosses the La Baume stream and turns left on to the alley which skirts it; after a few metres on the N464, the main street, continue straight ahead on the inn road, pass by the front of the Moulinot sawmill and at the fork, bear right and cross the stream. The path goes into the Ouche Wood, turns immediately right and continues flanking the hillside up to Sancey-le-Grand; it then descends and joins the Surmont road, arriving at Sancey-le-Grand.

Belvoir
The village is tucked away on the flank of a rocky, serrate ridge dominating the Sancey-le-Grand Valley; it is one of the few testaments to the Middle Ages preserved by Franche-Comté; a site of outstanding beauty, it offers many interesting sights for the visitor: to begin with, its 12th century château, one of the best preserved of the medieval period; it was restored by M. Jouffroy, a famous painter. It has a tower decorated with a curious, grotesque figure, called Mâge-Fâ. Then there are the ancient halls, which have also been recently restored, as well as 14th century houses; among these, an inn preserved in its original state, whose two monumental chimnies of the 12th and 16th centuries, as well as a superb Louis XIII staircase are particularly notable.

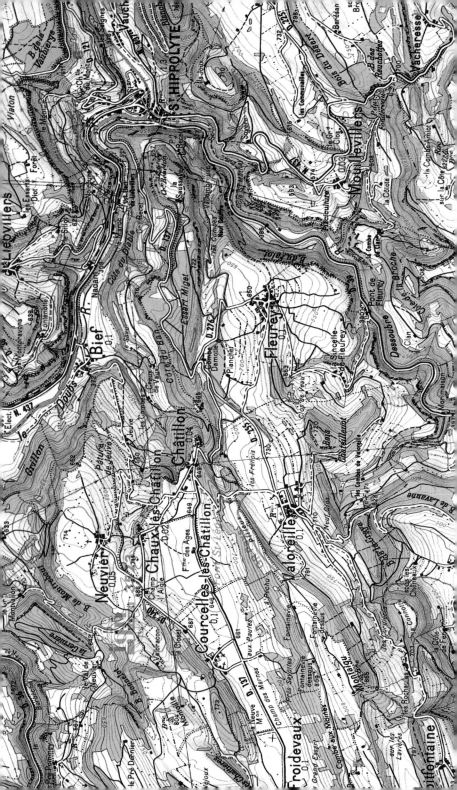

SANCEY-LE-GRAND
⌂ ✕ ▦

510m

There are some beautiful old houses in Sancey-le-Grand, here a tower, there a Roman arch; they withstood the Swedish siege of Saxe-Weimar in 1639. The art lover will discover plenty of other testimonies to the past: lattice windows, the escutcheons of great families now extinct, the monumental chimney of the Roussel restaurant. Going up the village, you discover the old lime tree of Sully, still standing after 400 years.

7.5Km
2:00

Picnic area with view of whole Sancey-le-Grand Valley, Château de Belvoir, and Lomont range.

Surmont
675m

5Km
1:15

BELLEHERBE
⌂ ✕ ⚖

745m

Belleherbe is situated on much the same latitude as

In the village, climb the D31 and, on the first bend, follow the road left so as to skirt the Dard stream and enter a beech grove. The path cuts across the stream, skirts round the cliff and reaches the "Rocher du Dard" view point.

Take the road left for 500 metres and enter a pasture on the right to avoid a bend in the road; climb across the pasture, cut across the D31 and descend the track which leads to the farm below. Before the farm, go right and into the meadow to arrive at a forest track in the Georgeot Combe locality. Follow this track eastwards, skirting the Côte Noire Wood. The track turns north to reach Surmont.

The GR crosses the village, passes in front of the church and reaches the fields by a gravelled track which, a little further on, bends to the left; leave this track and continue through fields towards the summit of the hill in a south easterly direction; in this way, you reach the upper plateau. The path joins a small road, turns left to the nearby farm, climbs again towards the wooded ridge behind it, and shortly afterwards, leaves the wood to continue along the bottom of a particularly peaceful and isolated combe leading to Ebey. Cross the hamlet and turn left on to the D32, towards Belleherbe.

The GR leaves the town reaching the Crêt de la Fin, where it takes a forest lane giving a beautiful view over the Doubs below, which joins the D343; turn left, turn on to the second road left and continue as far as the Valbirin

Maiche and, consequently, already belongs to the Haut-Doubs. The walker will realise this because of the forest cover of spruce, with some firs and deciduous trees. The village church possesses three very valuable paintings, representing respectively the martyrdom of St Sebastian, the Assumption of the Holy Virgin and the Death of St Joseph.

18Km
4:30

farm; climb the combe right to Moines for 3 kilometres to the Montaigu view-point at 820m.

Picnic area; views; north, Doubs Valley, Lomont and Montbéliard Region plateaux; south east, Dessoubre Valley and Maîche Plateau.

The GR continues over the pasture in a north easterly direction and comes out on to the old road from Valoreille to Châtillon-sous-Maîche, by the Saint-Léger fountain; it continues to descend the meadow below as far as the D137.

Detour *10 mins*
Château de Châtillon
Follow the D137 road left. Situated on rocky spur, it dominates Doubs Valley; feudal centre of the Sous-Maîche Plateau in hands of "La Roche Saint-Hippolyte".

The GR itself takes the D137 right, then turns on to the first field track right, to reach the D225 which it takes left or north. At the edge of the forest, take the forest path right which leads to the Fleury road. Take the track left at the hairpin bend, to descend the Combes and arrive at the ruins of Le Petit Recet. The path descends, right, to Saint-Hippolyte.

SAINT-HIPPOLYTE
⌂ 🏃 ✖ 🚉 🚌
380m
Situated at the junction of the Doubs and Dessoubre Valleys, at the foot of wooded escarpments and is the northern part of the Haut-Doubs. Rich in medieval history, it has kept its ancient "cachet", a 12th century house with a curious corbelling; a 14th century church, the Collégiale Notre-Dame; a former Ursuline convent.

After the bridge over the Doubs, the Regional GR takes the Montécheroux road, then passes behind the station.

Detour *5 km*
From this point, you can

Past the station, the Regional GR turns right on to a path behind the houses. As it climbs, this

5Km
1:15

reach the Tremblois Farm directly via Chamesol, without passing through Soulce-Cernay. To do this, make a detour climbing up as far as the Saint-Hippolyte cemetery, then from here, follow the red and white waymarking of the GR5 northwards. This section of the GR5, described from north to south, appears in Walk 2.

The Montbéliard Regional GR and the GR5 follow the same route as far as Soulce-Cernay; red and white waymarking.

Here, you leave the red and white waymarking of the GR5, which crosses the bridge and heads for Courtefontaine. You follow once again the red and yellow waymarking of the Regional GR.

SOULCE-CERNAY
✗
390m

6Km
2:00

Tremblois farm
The GR5 arrives from Saint-Hippolyte and Chamesol by the road from the left and the GR5 and the Regional GR again take the same route as far as Vandoncourt with red and white waymarkings.

THE LOMONT

path proceeds to the locality of Les Seignes and, a little further up, it joins the GR5 on a track from the left, near the D121.

Follow this track, right, as far as the Grosse Roche. Past this farm, descend, right, towards the bottom of the valley. The Regional GR does not cross the Doubs. Before the bridge, it continues on a road climbing to the north.

Here, the Regional GR takes a small road north and stays on it as far as the third "Sapois" farm; here, turn left behind the farm and climb up again against the cliff. You reach the Chamesol Plateau through a col by the Aiguille de Sapois. Then, by the Combe Auchy, the Combe au Saint and La Combotte, you join the little road from Villars-les-Blamont to Chamesol which you cross near the Tremblois farm.

Past the Tremblois farm, the GR passes the Fort du Lomont on the left and climbs to the ridge where it joins the strategic road.

On the strategic road on the ridge, if you turn left, you head for this monument and are then

---

The Lomont

This is a transverse mountain range with Jurassian folds, stretching over forty or so kilometres, from Clerval in the Doubs Valley to the Roche d'Or in Switzerland.

This was one of the eyries of the French Resistance during the Second World War and especially in 1944; the *maquisards* occupying the fort (currently, military property) received their arms and munitions there by parachute. They were very active in their preparations for the Belfort Gap attack. The imposing monument on the road from Montécheroux to Pierrefontaine-les-Blamont commemorates the fierce battles of August 1944 on the slopes of the Lomont.

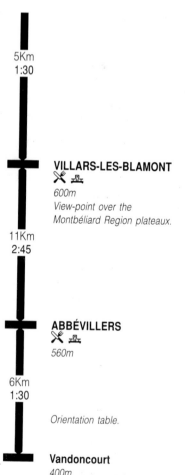

5Km
1:30

VILLARS-LES-BLAMONT

600m
*View-point over the
Montbéliard Region plateaux.*

11Km
2:45

ABBÉVILLERS

560m

6Km
1:30

Orientation table.

Vandoncourt
400m

on the 8 kilometre long scenic Lomont route descending to Pierrefontaine-les-Blamont. The GR takes the strategic road right and meets old military batteries and gives a panorama to the North over Alsace, the Vosges, and Montbéliard Region, and to the south, over the Jura and Switzerland. By a path at the edge of the Courbot wood, you reach the road, which you go downhill on as far as the village of Villars-les-Blamont.

The path crosses the N73 in the village and climbs the small Dannemarie road again as far as the last farmhouse; turn right here to arrive at the heights and the Swiss frontier; skirt this as far as the 380 boundary marker, then descend the valley to the left which leads to La Papeterie Inn. The GR continues parallel to the Doue stream, goes into the pasture left and climbs a wooded slope again to arrive on the plateau near some ruins. The GR then bears north to reach Abbévillers.

Cut across the road going towards Swizerland and leave the locality along the Montbouton road; at the Six Chemins crossroads, follow the tarmac then gravelled road which leads to the Hollard Forest; go into it. You soon find the Sarrazin Bridge lost amid the greenery. The GR takes the alternative GR5 route by the Roche Piquante view point to reach the town of Vandoncourt.

ACCOMMODATION GUIDE

The many different kinds of accommodation in France are explained in the introduction. Here we include a selection of hotels and other addresses, which is by no means exhaustive – the hotels listed are usually in the one-star or two-star categories. We have given full postal addresses where available so bookings can be made.

There has been an explosive growth in bed and breakfast facilities (chambres d'hôte) in the past few years, and staying in these private homes can be especially interesting and rewarding. Local shops and the town hall (mairie) can usually direct you to one.

Aubre
68150 Aubre
⌂
☎ *89.73.91.04*

Bagenelles, Col des
68160 Sainte-Marie-aux-Mines
⌂ *du Club Vosgien*
2 Croix de la Mission
M. André Schmitt
☎ *89.58.76.31*

Ballon d'Alsace
90200 Ballon d'Alsace
⌂ *du Ballon d'Alsace*
☎ *84.29.03.94*
⌂
E. Grunenwald
☎ *84.29.32.66*

Barr
67140 Barr
⌂
Rue du Dr. Sultzer
J.L. Bachert
☎ *88.08.95.89*

Belacker
68960 Belacker
⌂
Gustave Knibiehly
☎ *89.82.34.20*

Bois d'Amont
39220 Les Rousses
⌂
Mme Vandel
☎ *84.60.50.41*

Calvaire du Lac Blanc
⌂
☎ *89.71.31.31*

Chaffaud, Le
25130 Villers-le-Lac
⌂ *du CAF de Montbéliard*
☎ *81.68.12.55*

Chapelle des Bois
25240 Mouthe
⌂ *l'Acceuil Montagnard*
☎ *81.69.26.19*

Châtenois
67730 Châtenois
⌂
98 Rue du Maréchal Foch
M. Wasseur
☎ *88.92.26.20*

Climbach
67510 Climbach
⌂
2 Rue Soultz
Rott Robert
☎ *88.94.45.36*

Cluse-et-Mijoux, La
25300 Pontarlier
⌂ *du Château de Joux*
☎ *81.39.06.68*

Dabo
57850 Dabo
⌂
3 Rue des Jardins
Anstett Edmond
☎ *87.07.44.52*

Devin, Etang du
68650 Etang du Devin
⌂
Lapoutroie
Thérèse Bedez
☎ *89.47.20.29*

Fessevillers
25470 Trévillers
⌂
☎ *81.44.43.07*

Fort du Larmont Supérieur
25300 Pontarlier
⌂ *des Eclaireurs de France*
BP31
25300 Pontarlier
☎ *81.39.11.25*

Fourgs, Les
25300 Pontarlier
⌂
☎ *81.39.14.43*
⌂ *l'Orgière*
☎ *81.39.18.15*

Grand Ballon
68760 Grand Ballon
⌂
☎ *89.76.83.35*

Gruckert, Le
⌂ *des Amis de la Nature*
(Section de Strasbourg)
M. Xavier Breck
11d Rue de la Tuilerie
67100 Strasbourg
☎ *88.44.43.14*

Grand-Mont, Le
25790 les Gras
⌂
M. Jouille
☎ *81.68.82.10*

Granges Bailly
25300 Pontarlier
⌂
M. Pierre Beyeler

☎ *81.69.40.62*

Gros Morond
25300 Pontarlier
⌂ *du CAF de Pontarlier*
☎ *81.49.91.92/81.59.30.26*

Hahnenbrunnen, Col du
⌂ *du Touring Club de*
Mulhouse
Mme Marie-José Schwimmer
2 Place du Centre
68950 Reininque
☎ *89.81.90.76*

Hohwald, Le
67140 Le Hohwald
⌂
☎ *88.08.33.47*

Jougne
25370 les Hôpitaux-Neufs
⌂ *M. Polonghini*
☎ *81.49.12.70/81.49.13.02*

Lachapelle-sous-Chaux
90300
⌂
Rue du Rhône
☎ *84.29.23.74*

Lichtenberg
67340 Lichtenburg
⌂
Impasse de la Mairie
☎ *88.89.94.07*

Loge de Beauregard
39220 Prémanon
⌂
M. Gauthier
☎ *84.60.77.14*

Miroirs, Les
25300 Pontarlier
⌂ *Le Goune Fay*
Route du Larmont
☎ *81.39.05.99*

Molkenrain
68140 Molkenrain
⌂
J.P. Deybach
☎ *89.81.17.66*

Montbenoît
25650 Montbenoît
⌂ *La Grosse Grange*
M. Boucard
☎ *81.38.11.61*

Mont Jean
90200
⌂
Bernard Stalber
☎ *84.27.13.95*

Mouthe
25240 Mouthe
⌂ *la Randonnée*
Grande Rue
☎ *81.69.21.69*
⌂ *C Sources du Doubs*
☎ *81.69.27.61*

Oberbronn
67110 Oberbronn
⌂
C Eichelgarten
☎ *88.09.71.96*

Obersteinbach
67510 Obersteinbach
⌂
44 Rue Principale
Evelyne Berring
☎ *88.09.55.26*

Perdrix, La
25650 Montbenoît
⌂
Hauterive la Fresse
☎ *81.39.20.10*

Petits Fourgs, Les
25300 Pontarlier
⌂
M. Long
☎ *81.39.36.25 / 81.39.03.61*

Petit Morond
25370 les Hôpitaux-Neufs
⌂
M. Antoine Salvi
☎ *81.39.38.62*
(weekends, winter)

Pissoux, Le
25130 Villers-le-Lac
⌂
Lamy Family
☎ *81.43.76.74*

Rouge Gazon
88560 Rouge Gazon
🏠 ⌂
F. Luttenbacher
☎ *29.25.12.80*

Rousses, Les
39220 Les Rousses

⌂ *Le Grand Tétras*
☎ *84.60.51.13*

Schiessrothried, Lac du
⌂ *des Vosges Trotters de*
Colmar
M. Fernand Feuerstein
16 Avenue de l'Europe
68000 Colmar
☎ *89.41.10.33*

Sur la Roche
25130 Villers-le-Lac
⌂
☎ *81.68.08.94*

Tinfronce
68160
⌂ *Tinfronce*
René Petitdemange
☎ *89.58.76.61*

Trois Fours
68140
⌂ *des Trois Fours*
André Schott
☎ *89.77.31.14*

Touillon-et-Loutelet
25370 les Hôpitaux-Neufs
⌂ *MJC de Touillon-et-Loutelet*
☎ *81.49.10.04*

Vandoncourt
25230 Seloncourt
⌂
Chez M. Humbert
☎ *81.34.39.43*

Vaudey, Le
25140 Charquemont
⌂
☎ *81.44.07.57*

Vieux-Chateleu
25790 les Gras
⌂
☎ *81.67.11.59*

Villers-le-Lac
25130 Villers-le-Lac
⌂ *la Petite Ferme*
Route de Morteau
Mme Frantz
☎ *81.68.08.33*
⌂ *Centre de Vacances LVT*
Les Vergers
☎ *81.68.02.89*

Temps	LOCALITÉS / RESSOURCES	Pages	⌂	🏠	🏢	⛺	🛒	🍴	🚌	🚆
	GR 53 WISSEMBOURG	17			•	•	•	•	•	•
2.25	CLIMBACH	17		•	•		•	•		
5.40	OBERSTEINBACH	23		•	•		•	•	•	
5.15	NIEDERBRONN-LES-BAINS	25		•	•	•	•	•	•	•
5.35	LICHTENBERG	29		•	•		•	•		
1.15	WIMMENAU	29			•		•	•	•	•
1.40	ERCKARTSWILLER	29					•	•		
1.20	LA PETITE-PIERRE	31		•	•		•	•	•	
1.45	GRAUFTHAL	31			•		•	•		
0.45	OBERHOF	31			•			•		
2.30	SAVERNE	33		•	•	•	•	•	•	•
6	DABO	37	•		•	•	•	•	•	
2.20	WANGENBOURG	39		•	•		•	•	•	
3.45	OBERHASLACH	41			•		•	•		
0.45	URMATT	41			•		•	•		•
6	PLATE-FORME DU DONON	43			•			•		
2	GR 5 SCHIRMECK	43			•	•	•	•		•
6	LE HOHWALD	47		•	•	•	•	•		
2.45	MONT SAINTE-ODILE	49						•		
2.30	BARR	49		•	•		•	•		•
1	ANDLAU	49			•		•	•	•	
1	GRUCKERT	51	•							
5.15	HUEHNELMUEHLE	53			•			•		
0.45	CHATENOIS	53		•	•		•	•	•	
3.20	THANNENKIRCH	55			•		•	•		
1.25	RIBEAUVILLE	55			•	•	•	•		•
3	AUBURE	57		•	•	•	•	•		
3.15	COL DES BAGENELLES	59	•							
0.35	LE BONHOMME	59			•		•	•	•	
0.40	ETANG DU DEVIN	59		•				•		
1.45	REFUGE TINFRONCE	61	•					•		
1.10	GAZON DU FAING	63						•		
2.10	COL DE LA SCHLUCHT	63			•			•	•	
1.50	LAC DU SCHIESSROTHRIED	65	•							
1.15	METZERAL	65			•		•	•	•	•
0.45	MITTLACH	67			•	•	•	•		
3.15	COL DE HAHNENBRUNNEN	67	•							
1	MARKSTEIN	67			•			•		
2.05	GRAND-BALLON	69			•			•		
5.15	THANN	73			•		•	•	•	•
2.40	COL DU ROSSBERG	73	•							
0.50	FERME-AUBERGE BELACKER	75						•		
4.25	BALLON D'ALSACE	77	•		•			•		
3.10	GIROMAGNY	79			•	•	•	•	•	
1.20	LA CHAPELLE-SOUS-CHAUX	81						•	•	
1	EVETTE-SALBERT	81				•	•	•	•	•
2	CHALONVILLARS	85					•	•	•	
1.30	ECHENANS	85						•		
0.45	BREVILLIERS	85						•	•	
1.40	CHATENOIS-LES-FORGES	87			•		•	•	•	
0.25	NOMMAY	87						•	•	
1.25	FESCHES-LE-CHATEL	87			•		•	•	•	

INDEX

Details of bus/train connections have been provided wherever it was possible. We suggest you refer also to the map inside the front cover.

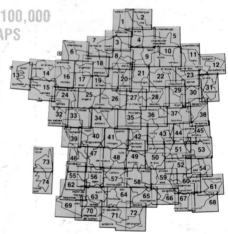
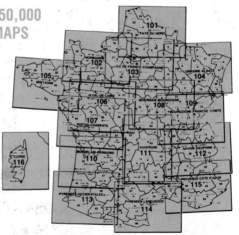